The Proven Track of Significance

Dr. Bob Abramson

The Proven Track of Significance
Dr. Bob Abramson

Cover design by Ryan Stacey

You may contact Dr. Abramson at dr.bob@mentoringministry.com or through his website: www.mentoringministry.com.

Contents

When I began writing, I had a heartwarming memory with which to start. It was powerful and perfectly suited to be developed into something meaningful. Here's the memory from which the beginnings of the book came forth.

The Light Will Surely Come.

When two of our five girls, Debby and Sarah, were very young, I took them to Disney World in Florida. I don't remember much about that particular time, except one thing - the dreaded Space Mountain! It's a roller coaster ride inside a dark structure that's made to look like a mountain. When you enter Space Mountain on the coaster, you find it's absolutely pitch black for the length of the entire ride. Now, most people love roller coasters and have a great time on this particular ride. However, until that day at Space Mountain, my personal policy was never to ride a roller coaster, as the sudden ups and downs make me physically ill.

Well, this was the only time I ignored that policy. Debby and Sarah wanted so badly to go on the ride. What could I do, except agree to take them on it? When we finally finished this seemingly endless trip through the darkness of my personal terror and discomfort (though the ride really only lasted a few brief minutes), I staggered out of Space Mountain into the daylight. I was barely able to get to the first available bench near the entrance. There I sat, feeling dizzy and quite sick, watching my two girls squealing with joy over how much they enjoyed the ride!

There are two points to my story. First, God never promised us that everything in life would be an enjoyable, comfortable ride. However, He does promise that regardless of how dark the ride may seem, it will end with our coming into the light. We just have to hang on, knowing the light at the end of the experience will surely come. My second point is that, as I look back at that ride through Space Mountain so many years ago, I see it as a gift from God, one that's a pure treasure. It was a memory I will cherish forever and it left an indelible mark on my heart. I have those memories of a very special time with two of my daughters as little girls. Every father knows that there is nothing better than that! It was truly a gift from God and a blessing of the greatest value. My only regret, as with many parents, is that I didn't understand the significance of giving my kids even more of my time and love. Those days with my young children went fleetingly by and were gone in a flash. Suddenly, they were grown.

"He is no fool who gives what he cannot keep to gain what he cannot lose."[1]

"He is wise who sees the significance of what should be cherished today without waiting for tomorrow."[2]

---

[1] Jim Elliot, martyred missionary.
[2] My thought, upon reflection (meant to be inclusive of both genders).

As you read "The Proven Track of Significance" you will find yourself on a journey toward understanding what brings significance to your life - the times, memories and the treasures given you. I pray that you will gain understanding of the treasures you have now, and of that most wonderful one that awaits you. Look at the definition of significance, below. Then, begin your journey through the book.

The Definition of Significance
(Merriam Webster.com)

"having meaning... likely to have influence or effect... important (as in: a significant piece of legislation); also: of a noticeably or measurably large amount... probably caused by something other than mere chance"

Consider the Christian perspective of this portion of Merriam Webster's definition of significance: "probably caused by something other than mere chance." We could interpret this conclusion as not "something," but "Someone," knowing God's hand is in it.

Significance in the life of a Christian has eternal meaning and does not come because of chance. It comes because God has a plan and a person. He sets the plan in motion as He appoints and anoints the person to bring it to pass. It's a "cause and effect" event that has supernatural, heavenly origins and eternally significant meaning. May you gain insight into the lasting imprints you make and experience each day, as you walk with God down "The Proven Track of Significance."

The Significance of Time

ONE

Time Never Stands Still.

Ecclesiastes 3:1-8

*"To everything there is a season, A time
for every purpose under heaven:"*

As I write this, I'm in the seventieth year of life. I'm eternally grateful for who the Lord has been in my life and what He has done for me. To tell about this would be an endless effort and it's not my purpose to try. Instead, let's focus on the common denominator we all face. It's the one thing that's irreversible and to which we can all look forward. Of course, it's the perpetual march of time.

Every season of time and life has a beginning and end. We only have a limited time to leave our mark on the world. Every moment holds the potential for us to leave positive or negative marks of significance. Each of us should ask what kind of significance we want to leave when we are gone. We also should consider how open we will be to the marks others might make on our hearts. Having a grateful and teachable attitude is a believer's privilege. In the time we have, we should see its value and do what we can to take advantage of its opportunities.

Here's an even more important question to ask ourselves: What kind of mark will we have left on the heart of the

Lord Jesus Christ, who is our Lord, Savior… and yes, our Judge? The end of life is not the end. There's an endless season in eternity awaiting us. It holds divinely given rewards for us that will wholly depend on the marks we leave as our legacies.

Matthew 16:27

"For the Son of Man will come in the glory of His Father with His angels, and then He will reward each according to his works."

Landmarks in Time

Every moment provides you with an opportunity to grow and change. Every moment also provides you an opportunity to recognize and embrace those people who are your gifts from God. Make good memories of the moments you have to share with them. Turn these into blessings that become the marks of your life. These will become landmarks - landmarks of light beyond the moment. They will shine for eternity.

I have fond memories of my weekly trips to the grocery with my mother when she was in the latter years of her life. These were necessary for her to stock up on food for the week, but that was not why I was there with her. We spent about two hours shopping each week, and we both got something very special out of walking the aisles together. It was almost like a return to when I was growing up. In those days, long since past, we spent wonderful times gardening in our little back yard. Though about forty years passed between my gardening as a child to our shopping trips in her latter days, I found them amazingly similar. Both were truly special gifts with a special lady, from our very special God.

Looking back, these many years after my mom died, I still have a precious, warm feeling inside when the memories of the gardening or shopping come to me. These times will always be landmarks of light and will shine for eternity. What are your landmark memories? They can still speak to you and provide you with warmth and gratitude inside. They hold the potential to cause you to thank God for what could easily be forgotten or taken for granted. They are landmarks of God's grace. They are landmarks of His kind of love. Thank Him for them and let them continue to speak to you about His goodness.

A Lifetime is but a Moment.

Have you ever lit a match and watched it flame up for a brief moment and then quickly darken? I remember, as a kid, trying to light a fire in our home's fireplace on a cold wintery day. I laid the wood on the old sooty structure in the fireplace. Then I crumpled newspaper and put it under the wood. The trick to all this was to get the paper to catch before the burning match flamed out, darkened and died. If I paid enough attention and had enough dexterity, I could get the flame to ignite the paper. It only took a brief moment, so I had to be quick. Then the flame went from the paper to the wood, and with a little encouragement, I could get a roaring fire going. Then, I could bask in the heat. It was a good feeling. What beautiful memories!

A lifetime is but a moment. We all need to understand this and ignite something fruitful and filled with significance in our lives that will burn on long after we're gone. Think about this and ask yourself what you can ignite that might make a difference in someone else's life, perhaps even in their eternity.

If you have been around me, you have probably heard me say, *"I'm on fire and the devil is a liar!"* That's because there's a fire burning in my spirit that desires to ignite something for Jesus. It just wants to flame up and warm somebody's life! What about you? Will you be combustible for Jesus while there's still time? A lifetime is really but a brief moment.

A Moment Can Change a Lifetime

It was in the early Nineteen-Nineties. I was part of a ministry team and I was speaking to a graduating class at a Bible school in Fiji. In the class were people who were about to go to remote, distant mission fields across the South Pacific in what we would call "hard places." It would be difficult and in some cases dangerous for them. There was a young man there that day, whom I had the opportunity to speak over publicly with some prophetic words of encouragement. I can't remember his name, and certainly don't remember what I said. It has been too many years.

I had long forgotten this moment in time. Then, a few years back, I got a letter from the young man. He wrote that he was still on the mission field in the South Pacific. (I had since returned to America.) When I first read the letter, I had no idea who he was. As I read further, he reminded me of that moment in time in Fiji when I spoke words over him. Here's a paraphrase of what he wrote.

> "I never forgot the words you spoke over me. I have kept them in my heart all these years. It has been really tough and many times I wanted to quit. I want you to know that your words have kept me going and I am determined as ever to keep on with the work of the Lord."

It was apparently a moment in his life that became a treasure of significance that changed him forever. It was a God-glorifying, devil horrifying moment in which the Holy Spirit burned a few intentionally edifying words into this young man so he could run his race with excellence and not deny his destiny. I am grateful that God saw it fitting to reward me with his letter. As I read it, I knew it was purposefully appointed from God to remind me of the importance of igniting others with a fiery zeal for Jesus. It was also one of those significant moments when God said to me, "Well done."

No Extra Innings, No Overtime Opportunities

Time never waits for anyone. It just keeps on marching. At the appointed time, we all end our brief stay on this earth. Unless God intervenes, it's impossible to stretch the limits of our lifetimes. This means that we need to value and take advantage of the time we have. Unlike football, basketball, baseball, rugby or so many other sports, there are no second chances, no extra innings or overtime periods to do one more thing. When it comes to our opportunities to make a difference, we have to give it our all, because time runs out. There are no half-hearted fence sitters who make a significant difference in the kingdom of God. Being lukewarm throughout our lives also means experiencing the disappointment and displeasure of the Lord. He makes this clear in the strongest of terms. He says, *"because you are lukewarm, and neither cold nor hot, I will vomit you out of My mouth."*

Revelation 3:14-16

"And to the angel of the church of the Laodiceans write, 'These things says the Amen, the Faithful and True Witness, the Beginning of the creation of God: {15} "I know your works, that you are neither cold nor hot. I could wish you were cold or hot. {16} So then, because you are lukewarm, and neither cold nor hot, I will vomit you out of My mouth."

Thinking we can get by in life by remaining *"lukewarm"* for Christ is to fool ourselves concerning the inevitable outcomes we will face. There will surely be more sorrows and regrets than we expected or planned on. To accept the truths of God's Word and the call to fulfill them means to take the challenge and refuse to be denied the chance to be a blessing.

Every committed Christian will face a lifetime of spiritual warfare. The great lie is that it will not happen! The truth is, God's Word declares that part of your life's experience will be to battle demonic forces for your victories. There's to be nothing *"lukewarm"* about it.

1 Corinthians 10 4-5

"For the weapons of our warfare are not carnal but mighty in God for pulling down strongholds, {5} casting down arguments and every high thing that exalts itself against the knowledge of God, bringing every thought into captivity to the obedience of Christ,"

God has given you the means to win your battles. Your spiritual weapons are more than sufficient, because the Holy Spirit has filled them with power. Christ's death on the cross has already gained the victory for you.

Numbers 23:19

"God is not a man, that He should lie, Nor a son of man, that He should repent. Has He said, and will He not do? Or has He spoken, and will He not make it good?"

Don't Fellowship with the Wrong Memories.

As followers of Christ, we have left behind the darkness of unbelief and now live in God's light. If we are to use our time to make a significant mark in the lives of others, we have to leave behind any longing for or treasuring of dark memories from the past. They're gone forever. We have been delivered. The Bible instructs us to create new and wonderful memories. We do this by consistently demonstrating the love of God toward others.

Ephesians 5:1-2

"Therefore be imitators of God as dear children.
²And walk in love, as Christ also has loved us
and given Himself for us, an offering and a
sacrifice to God for a sweet-smelling aroma."

As imitators of God, we are to give evidence of the new memories we've made from living in the Lord's marvelous gifts of life and light.

Ephesians 5:8, 11, 13-17

"For you were once darkness, but now you are
light in the Lord. Walk as children of light...
{11} And have no fellowship with the unfruitful
works of darkness, but rather expose them...
{13} But all things that are exposed are made
manifest by the light, for whatever makes
manifest is light. {14} Therefore He says:

"Awake, you who sleep, Arise from the
dead, And Christ will give you light."

{15} See then that you walk circumspectly, not
as fools but as wise, {16} redeeming the time,
because the days are evil. {17} Therefore do not
be unwise, but understand what the will of the
Lord is."

When I was first gave my life to Christ, my profession was in the field of architectural design. Following my salvation experience, I knew immediately that God was calling me into full-time ministry, but I still had clients whom I was obligated to service. One of them was a homebuilder, with whom I had a contract to do some design work. At the completion of the contract, I went to his office to collect my fees. My wife, Nancy, accompanied me. When we sat down at the man's desk, he told us he was not going to pay for the services we had provided. He said he had no reason, except that he did not want to part with the money.

I had every right to be paid what I was owed. Had this happened prior to my salvation experience, I would have reacted in anger, spoken some very harsh words, and taken the man to court. Now, I saw things differently. I reacted by remembering God was now my source and I chose to trust Him. I spoke to the man with politeness, confirming that he would not relent. Then, I told Nancy we were leaving. We did so, and have never looked back. I surrendered the anger and retribution into God's hands. I have never regretted the decision.

To this day I have not coveted or missed the thousands of dollars I was owed. God has faithfully supplied all of our needs through the years Nancy and I have served Him as missionaries and ministers of the Gospel. I know this was a test of whether I would trust God and not return to the darkness I left behind. When I gave this entire challenging experience to God, I think I passed the test. Time has marched on and my memories now are fixed on the good things we experienced in the many years that followed that incident. I write of it only to testify to the goodness of God. He may not direct you to walk away from what is rightly yours, but He will surely provide for you when you make the deliberate choice to walk in the light. Remember what He's done for you. Anticipate what He will do for you. Expect it. Believe Him for it. He is faithful.

Philippians 4:19

"And my God shall supply all your need according to His riches in glory by Christ Jesus our Lord."

There will be times when you experience unfair treatment. When this happens to you, there will be the temptation and the opportunity to let your emotions seize control of the situation. However, when you walked out of the darkness into God's marvelous light, you left behind your old life. You began a new one. There's a large quantity of biblical instruction regarding how you should behave in your new life as a Christian. Below, I have selected Scripture from Colossians, Chapter 3 and recorded my thoughts about it to help provide you with specific instructions in how to create good, God pleasing memories.

New Thinking for the "New Man" - Practical Instructions from Colossians, Chapter 3

Verses 1-2

"If then you were raised with Christ, seek those things which are above, where Christ

is, sitting at the right hand of God. {2} Set your mind on things above, not on things on the earth."

We are to look up toward God in those times when we're treated unfairly or suffer persecution. Paul encourages us to draw on the heavenly wisdom that God's Word provides, and not be tempted to be drawn back to the worldly ways we used to think.

"Put to death" and *"Put off"*

Verse 5

"Therefore put to death your members which are on the earth: fornication, covetousness, passion, evil desire, and covetousness, which is idolatry."

The expression *"put to death"* dictates that we are to take violent action to kill the thinking that formerly controlled our lives. Paul gives us a short list of what to *"put to death."* It's only partial. It's meant to provide examples of the many lusts of the flesh that are characteristic of the old life we left behind. Our new memories, gifts and blessings come from the new life in Christ we now enjoy. Are you thinking with a renewed mind - *"the mind of Christ,"* so you can give evidence of this? (Romans 12:2 and 1 Corinthians 2:16)

The expression *"put off"* implies an aggressive, deliberate act.

Verses 8-9

> *"But now, you yourselves are to put off all these: anger, wrath, malice, blasphemy, unclean language out of your mouth. {9} Do not lie to one another, since you have put off the old man with his deeds,"*

In Verses 8-9, Paul adds to the list. He emphasizes that nobody else can make the changes inside of you except you. His focus is on two issues in these verses. First, he says to reject the worldly, evil emotions and the words that go with them. Just put them off! Then he says to avoid lying because it's an act of the *"old man,"* who is now dead. You have crucified him (Galatians 2:20).

"Put on" and *"do."*

Verses 10, 12-13

> *"and have put on the new man who is renewed in knowledge according to the image of Him who created him... {12} Therefore, as the elect of God, holy and beloved, put on tender mercies, kindness, humility, meekness, longsuffering; {13} bearing with one another, and forgiving one another, if anyone has a complaint against another; even as Christ forgave you, so you also must do."*

Paul's instructions concerning what we are to *"put on"* closely parallel Jesus' words in the Beatitudes (Matthew 5:1-10). The combined message of these Scriptures reinforces a powerful point. There can be no confusion or doubt as to how the *"new man"* should live and be seen by others.

As the *"elect of God,"* we are given the specifics of how to act concerning what must be *"put on."* Verse 13 plainly says, *"...so you also must do."* This is not a suggestion. It's not to be casually accepted. If ignored, it can become a rebuke to the actions of fence sitters or those in the *"lukewarm"* church. Remember, time doesn't stand still. Jesus is coming for a holy church.

"Above all these things"

Verses 14-15

"But above all these things put on love, which is the bond of perfection. {15} And let the peace of God rule in your hearts, to which also you were called in one body; and be thankful."

The New Testament always brings us back to the issue of God's love. You cannot go far into any of the gospels or epistles without some mention of it. Love remains the foundation of Christian living. Verse 14 tells us that putting on love is more important than all the other characteristics Paul has mentioned. Paul calls it *"the bond of perfection."* This may be paraphrased as *"the Christian maturity that keeps us connected to each other."* The subject of unity was never far from Paul's message to us. He had the mind of Christ. His desire was that we have God's love firmly within us, so it becomes our motivation to please God.

In Verse 15, Paul encourages us to surrender our hearts to be governed by God's peace. Paul saw the wisdom of having the peace of God as the foundation of the *"new man."* God's peace is our very present help throughout our lifetime of walking with God.

Verses 16-17

> *"Let the word of Christ dwell in you richly in all wisdom, teaching and admonishing one another in psalms and hymns and spiritual songs, singing with grace in your hearts to the Lord. {17} And whatever you do in word or deed, do all in the name of the Lord Jesus, giving thanks to God the Father through Him."*

Verse 16 instructs us to surround ourselves and our brothers and sisters in Christ with the wisdom and teaching of the Bible. We are to admonish one another through the use of liturgies that are part of our individual traditions. This means we are to lovingly remind one another to keep relying on God's wisdom through Christ's presence in us. This is to be taken as a way to edify or build up one another, so we become more like Jesus.

Verse 17 speaks to our actions. Whatever we say or do, regardless of how unimportant it may seem, should be said and done *"in the name of the Lord Jesus."* This admonition carries the weight of judging whether it's worthy of the name of the Lord. We are to think before we speak or act, allowing the Holy Spirit to help us measure the righteousness of our words and deeds. The verse ends by instructing us to remember to give thanks to God in the midst of our speech and actions.

Throughout these verses of Colossians Chapter 3, Paul has provided us with specific instructions on how to *"put off the old man"* and *"put on the new man."* These are significantly timeless guideposts for living. They will help us to make heart-warming, God-pleasing memories, as our limited time on earth moves steadily toward its conclusion. Time never stands still. God is watching and He always makes a way for us to use it wisely and with significance. Let this be your heart's desire. Let it be your legacy.

> "Yesterday is history.
> Tomorrow is a mystery.
> Today is a gift.
> That's why it's called the present!"[3]

> What will you do with your today?

---

[3] Numerous sources - origin unknown.

TWO

Redeem the Time.

To redeem means to purchase back what was given up or sold. It's to regain for a cost what was lost or wasted. It speaks of an opportunity for redemption. Our great example of this is God's plan of salvation. It began in the time of our first parents, Adam and Eve. They sold mankind into sin through their disobedience to God. In the fullness of time, Jesus paid the precious cost of His shed blood, suffering and death on the cross to redeem us. As a result, believers no longer live in a wasteland of wasted time. We've been bought with that invaluable price for a purpose - to glorify God in our redemption. This is accomplished as we steward our times and seasons in demonstration of God-pleasing kingdom living.

I have an indelible memory etched on my heart of stumbling into a church for all the wrong reasons and then quite to my surprise, walking the aisle and giving my life to Christ. I had no idea that it was to be the beginning of a significant season that would be completely foreign to how life had previously been for me. It was the beginning of my discovery of who God is and of finding out what He would do to completely transform my life. I already had enough tragedy for a lifetime; and so I chose to redeem the time God has given me in my new, born-again season of life. I determined to embrace God's plan for my life, even before I understood how radically different and fruitful it could be. I never regretted this choice. I have never looked back.

It has become a subject of my daily prayers to ask the Holy Spirit to impart wisdom to me that would help me avoid mistakes or foolishness that would waste the day's opportunities. Nevertheless, I'm sure I have much to learn about avoiding mistakes. I have accepted that, in my imperfect human nature, making mistakes is inevitable. Charles Spurgeon, with his mature perspective about life in Christ, had some wisdom to impart about this:

> "We look down into the abyss of error, and it almost makes our head swim to think of the perilous descent; but the road of the gospel, to which we hope to keep by divine grace, is a safe and happy way."[4]

You can be sure that in a season's beginnings you will not fully understand how the plan of God will unfold, nor what experiences, gifts and blessings may be waiting for you. You can also be sure that this will mostly depend on your willingness to open your heart and use the time to draw near to God. Otherwise, the experiences, gifts and blessings will be lost. They will be replaced with experiences that were never part of God's plan. Wasting these gifts and blessings would be a tragedy. The limits or boundaries for our lives leave a finite amount of time to be

---

[4] The Downgrade Controversy - First article P. 4.

fruitful. There are limited numbers of days to create a significant legacy of our redemption that honors Christ. Within this legacy, God has left plenty of room for the enjoyment of life and appreciation for the wonders of His creation. It's not supposed to be all work without moments of rest and leisure. Every moment is valuable and God desires that we redeem each of them for a full life's experience.

Think about how you are living life. What makes up a typical day or week for you? Is it balanced, enjoyable and productive? Or, is it unbalanced, stressful and without much satisfaction? Do you concern yourself with the well-being of those you are close to and with whom you ought to spend considerable quality time? If not, consider the opportunity you have to redeem what you've misspent or wasted.

The Balanced Christian Life of Faith

When it comes to redeeming the time, it can often be tricky trying to balance fervent faith with common sense. Unquestionably, faith should have the upper hand. However, there are times when God's people mistakenly discard common sense in the name of faith. Fervent faith will certainly go beyond common sense, but often, God desires it to work within the exercise of common sense. You can accomplish this by rethinking and reordering your priorities, so they fit with the biblical picture of a balanced, faith-filled life.

In one of my previous books, "Just a Little Bit More - The

Heart of a Mentor," I told of a significant encounter which stretched my faith beyond what common sense told me. Times and lives were redeemed.

> "One day, my Assistant Pastor in Fiji, Emitai, came to me and told me there was someone he wanted me to meet. We went to a storefront in downtown Suva. It was in a small office there, where I met Daniel.[5] He was sitting at a desk, reading his Bible. Daniel and Emitai had first met on the streets of Suva and Emitai led him to the Lord. Emitai then began to build a relationship with him. Daniel was eager to hear all Emitai had to say about Jesus.
>
> When Daniel met Emitai, it was Daniel's "road to Damascus" encounter. He was hungry for all he could learn about Jesus. So there I was, face to face with this unassuming new convert, who told me his story. I didn't know it at the time, but it would be the beginning of a God-ordained relationship between us. It would teach me not to put limitations on what I expected because of what common sense told me I saw in someone. (It's a lesson I seem to need reminding of every now and then.).
>
> Daniel was brilliant but had applied his brilliance to a career of dishonesty. Word travels fast in a small nation like Fiji. His reputation was ruined. He had defrauded a large number of

---

[5] The name has been changed.

people. It was common knowledge he could not be trusted. He was destitute because he could not be employed. Daniel told me he had been arrested for his dishonest dealings and was out on bond. He was scheduled to go to trial shortly. As I sat across from him that day, I listened politely and tried to encourage him. However, I held no great expectations for his future. Common sense dictated that he would be locked up and out of my life soon. I had seen others like him who said the right things because they were facing jail.

The next Sunday, Daniel brought his family to church. Over the weeks that followed, He and his wife were there every time the doors opened. He could be found praying and praising at every opportunity. I just knew time was running out for Daniel. In spite of his newfound Christianity, and apparent change of behavior, his time to go before the judge approached. We prayed with him for favor, but as I have said, I fully expected him to end up behind bars. I felt that once that happened, he would probably turn his back on God. Daniel admitted that he had done what he was accused of. He was finished… but nothing is ever finished unless Christ declares it is.

What happened in the courtroom defied logic. On the day of his trial, Daniel stood before the judge, and apologized to the court and to those he had swindled. He said something like this.

Your honor, I'm guilty of all that I am charged with. I'm willing to accept my punishment. I'm sorry for what I have done and ask for forgiveness. I have turned my life over to Christ, but I don't want to use that as an excuse to plead for leniency. I'm in your hands, but I want you to know that even in prison, I will serve the Lord with all my heart for the rest of my life.

The judge, against all logic and expectations (especially mine), told Daniel he had decided to dismiss all the charges! To this day, nobody knows why the judge did that. It could only have been the favor and grace of God speaking to the judge's heart. That day, Daniel walked out of court a free man. I have seen people get what they needed from God and then turn their backs on him. Daniel did just the opposite. His deliverance fired up his faith and stoked his zeal. He was literally on fire for God!

The story doesn't end there. Daniel showed up at my home one morning and I invited him into my office. He said he was going into business to become a financial advisor. He would do this within the same business community in which he had worked all his fraudulent activities. It was not even rational. Daniel said he was asking for my help for three reasons. First, I was his pastor. Second, he did not have a computer and I did. Third, he knew I had previous experience in business and he respected my wisdom and wanted my help. My initial thought was, *"This guy is nuts! How does he expect anyone to trust him and commit their funds to his care?"* My second thought was, *"Well, I'm his pastor and my job is to encourage him, so I will go along with him, even though this is a waste of time!"*

We subsequently met a couple times a week for months. Each time, we would craft a section of his business plan. When he next came to the house, he would bring a yellow legal pad with new ideas and notes handwritten on it. He continued in faith to move ahead with his plan. We would discuss what he had written and I would transform it to the computer, editing the language as I went. It became a very good business plan. Eventually we had a professional package he could use to make presentations. He took it and began trying to get people to engage him to guide their business investments.

I still believed he was wasting his time and mine. I thought he was naïve at best. Someone might listen to him out of politeness, but with his reputation, who would ever buy what he was selling?

Then one day he showed up at my door with a big smile on his face. Again we sat in my office. He told me he had proposed to a wealthy and successful businessman that he help him prepare a plan to fund a business to supply vegetables to the resorts on the island and for export to other nations around the world. The man agreed, knowing full well who Daniel was! There it was - the same favor and grace God placed on the judge. I was amazed. I repented for my lack of faith. Now we began to write the agreement for this new venture. I helped him with the necessary paperwork that followed. Looking back, I remember thinking, *"God, I don't have time for this. I'm trying to pastor a church and run a ministry training school."* All I heard in my spirit was, *"Yes you have time. Just do it."*

This became the first of many successful business ventures Daniel had. He became a pillar in the community, as well as in our church. He reestablished himself as completely trustworthy. The months turned into years, and he has provided very well for his family and continues to bless the church.

Daniel had been redeemed. His faith, combined with a common sense business plan, took him beyond what seemed possible. This was a lesson that took my faith to a new level. What I thought might have been time wasted was time redeemed. God makes all things possible to him who believes. Take it to the bank! Jesus is Lord. Have faith. Redeem your time while you can. Make it a successful transition into what God has prepared for you. Gain the redemptive treasure that has eternal value."

Ephesians 5:15-16

"See then that you walk circumspectly, not as fools but as wise, {16} redeeming the time, because the days are evil."

Clark's Commentary on Ephesians 5:16 says this: "Let time be your chief commodity; deal in that alone; buy it all up, and use every portion of it yourselves. Time is that on which eternity depends; in time ye are to get a preparation for the kingdom of God; if you get not this in time, your ruin is inevitable; therefore, buy up the time."[6]

The essential warning from Clark's Commentary may be paraphrased in this manner: "Pay close attention to the value of the time you are given. It's limited and should not be squandered. You may be assured of personal ruin if you don't redeem the time as preparation for your future in God's kingdom." This is a powerful, personally focused warning. When Paul wrote, *"See then that you walk circumspectly,"* he was warning, just as Clark's Commentary does, that we should move ahead in life with measured caution concerning how we utilize our time. We ought not play the fool with our opportunities. Time is indeed, a significant, irreplaceable gift from God and a treasure beyond an earthly price.

---

[6] Clark's Commentary on Ephesians 5:16; Online.

THREE

The In-Between Times

Transitions play a significant part in all of our lives. We can think of transitions from one season to the next as disruptions in the way things were on the way to how things are going to be. Because we are creatures of routine and find comfort in the certainty of repetitious and familiar patterns in our lives, transitions can be uncertain and unsettling. When these inevitable times of change come, they disrupt our routines and patterns. We tend to feel as if we've lost the safe, familiar footing that secures us. In these times our faith is seriously tested. It's as if we are hanging on by our fingers.

"Let Go of the Branch."

"A man was walking along a narrow path, not paying much attention to where he was going. Suddenly he slipped over the edge of a cliff. As he fell, he grabbed a branch growing from the side of the cliff. Realizing that he couldn't hang on for long, he called for help. He yelled, "Is anybody up there?" He heard a voice, "Yes, I'm here." The man responded, "Who is that?"

"THIS IS GOD!"

The man thought for a minute about what he just

> heard. Then, he replied, "Lord help me!" The voice then asked, "Do you trust Me?" Again, the man replied, "I trust you completely." Then the voice said, "Good. Let go of the branch!" "What???"
>
> "I said, 'Let go of the branch.'"
>
> There was a long pause. Finally, the man said, "Is anybody else up there?""[7]

I have often used this story while teaching and preaching to illustrate the tests of faith we all will face in some fashion. I used to wonder if I would let go of the branch, but my own experiences have shown I have done so. It was not always my favored choice, but trusting and obeying God became my only one. I have experienced a number of significant transitions, even life threatening ones, in which I found nothing left to hang onto except my faith. I had no other path to solid ground but to let myself fall into God's arms. If God says it, that's it! Whether or not you will let go is one of those questions that only personal experience will answer. When transitions come, and you have to release your grip on everything that has secured you, will you tightly grasp your faith in God? Will you let go of everything else? These are serious questions and may not easily be answered. Nevertheless, they're worth some serious thought.

---

[7] I have heard this story from a number of references. Among them, I have selected the following one: Michael P. Green, *Illustrations for Biblical Preaching* (Grand Rapids: Baker, 1989), Electronic Ed.

Faith's Challenge: Let Go and Get God.

There are always two significant issues in every transition. These issues will have profound effects on what comes next. First, there is the issue of the memories you won't let go of, and in your refusal, you drag into the transition. They need to be surrendered to the past or perhaps even die in the transition. Sometimes, you just have to find the faith to loosen your grip on them! Second, there's the issue of memories in the making. These are made from what you will find, accept and embrace as gifts from God that await you the transition. You will find these as you willingly fall into the arms of God, trusting Him to take you to your blessings. When there's nowhere else to go, take yourself to a place of anticipation of the impending goodness of God. Let's look at both of these issues.

The In-Between Times Require Letting Go.

I often think about how many years it took for Nancy and me to get over most of our feelings of having to leave Fiji. Our church there was beyond anything we could have expected. We had an incredibly successful ministry school and made wonderful lifelong friends. And then… it was finished. Away we went, back to America. Then there was nothing to hang onto except some of the best memories we will ever have. Everything else had slipped out of our grasp. There wasn't yet anything to look forward to. God had not yet put New York City in my heart. So here we were, back at our home church in Florida, feeling the loss, and in many ways, feeling lost.

After a time, God spoke and directed us to go to New York City. There, I was determined to duplicate what we had in Fiji. God, however, was determined to do something completely different. There was no arguing with God. If you could consider it a contest, guess who won? Guess who always wins? You're right - God! Time proved that being in the will of God is always a victory. I learned that what had to be released were two things. First, I had to release the longing for a return to what was finished. I had to give it up, look ahead and anticipate the inevitable supernatural intervention of God. Second, there was the memory of how it felt to be at the center of something so fulfilling and personally edifying. I realize now that these feelings took me to a place where I had trouble releasing the sense of personal importance and accomplishment I had owned for myself. It took this new season for me to learn that age-old lesson that I was not indispensible. In retrospect, it was purely a tussle with my pride. For a long time, my pride had the upper hand, but ultimately, I came to the place where I became settled in just being that "bondservant' of Jesus I professed to be. I began to identify with taking my place as that tiny little thread of blessing in the incredible coat of many colors that is the plan and purpose of God.

The Plans and Purposes of God

It makes little or no sense to try to define God's plans and purposes. It also makes absolutely no sense trying to defy them. God is too large and His plans and purposes are so much higher than our ability to understand very much of them. The best we can do is to surrender to His will, knowing that it's the only correct response... and the one that will bring blessings. In fact, it's a completely sensible response to the emotions our transitions dump on us. I have learned over and over again that it's not about me; it's about Him and His Kingdom. I have had to repeatedly embrace a Kingdom mentality and choose to empower it. This is a lesson we all seem to be given opportunities to learn, over and over. Think about your life. Perhaps you've resisted God's will, or perhaps you've made the decision to embrace it. I assure you that you will have the opportunity to make the choice. Be sure to make the one that says, "I surrender." It's the great opportunity we always find within the transitions of our lives.

His Ways Are Higher Than Ours.

Isaiah 55:8-11

"My thoughts are not your thoughts,
Nor are your ways My ways," says the Lord.
{9} "For as the heavens are higher than the earth,
So are My ways higher than your ways
And My thoughts than your thoughts.
{10} For as the rain comes down, and the snow
from heaven
And do not return there,
But water the earth,
And make it bring forth and bud,
That it may give seed to the sower
And bread to the eater,
{11} So shall My word be that goes forth from My
mouth; It shall not return to Me void,

But it shall accomplish what I please, And it shall prosper in the thing for which I sent it."

His Ways

When God says, *"My thoughts are not your thoughts, Nor are your ways My ways,"* and *"For as the heavens are higher than the earth, so are My ways higher than your ways And My thoughts than your thoughts,"* His words announce that there's a distance we cannot cross between His ways and our ways. This isn't about our failures or frailties. God simply is saying there will always be things He does that are so far above our ways of doing things that they are beyond our understanding. This should actually give us comfort and assurance. Because He's God, we can trust in how He does things.

Even though God's ways are so much higher than ours, He has provided us two means with which to understand enough of them to allow us to walk in the power, safety and significance they provide. The first way is found in His written Word - the Bible. What God has said in His Word is the raw material of a storehouse of wisdom we can obtain and carry with us. The second is found in the voice of the Holy Spirit. This requires us to obtain and then maintain an ever-growing personal relationship with Him. As we build this relationship, we are better able to recognize and understand His voice. Then, we can receive and walk in what He has to say. Essentially, God has given us, His children, a supernaturally enabled way to get beyond the distance we cannot naturally cross. It's part of the miracle of our salvation. The challenge is to reach out and establish a pattern of relationship with the Holy Spirit.

The wonderful thing about this relationship with the Holy Spirit is that when He speaks, either through His Word or in your relationship with Him, it will guarantee you can hear His will for you. This means it's going to be good for you. There's nothing hard about understanding this. However God accomplishes it, know that He is faithful and true. Look for His Word and listen for His voice. Today could be your day.

Today Could Be Your Day.

Isaiah 43:13 (NLT)

"From eternity to eternity I am God.
No one can snatch anyone out of my hand.
No one can undo what I have done."

Isaiah 43:18-19 (NLT)

"But forget all that -
it is nothing compared to what I am going to do.
{19} For I am about to do something new.
See, I have already begun! Do you not see it?
I will make a pathway through the wilderness.
I will create rivers in the dry wasteland."

You may have been through a season of great success and significance. Or, maybe you are transitioning out of what seemed like a personal wilderness and probably felt like a *"dry wasteland"* where there was no relief. In either case, transition affords you the opportunity for a fresh start. Today could be the time when God releases significant rivers of newness and perhaps the refreshing you have longed for. Treat Isaiah 43:18-19 as your personal promise from God. Then, take to heart the message in Isaiah 43:13. In the Amplified Bible, God said it this way, *"I will work and who can hinder or reverse it?"* Of course, the answer is nobody, because only God is God! If that's not quite enough, add one more thing from Scripture. Exercise the instructions in Palm 37.

The Key to the In-between Times

Psalm 37:1-6

A Psalm of David

"Do not fret because of evildoers,
  Nor be envious of the workers of iniquity.
{2} For they shall soon be cut down like the grass,
  And wither as the green herb.
{3} Trust in the Lord, and do good;
  Dwell in the land, and feed on His faithfulness.
{4} Delight yourself also in the Lord,
  And He shall give you the desires of your heart.
{5} Commit your way to the Lord,
  Trust also in Him,
  And He shall bring it to pass.
{6} He shall bring forth your righteousness as the light,
  And your justice as the noonday."

In spite of whatever it seems like, treat your transition as if it's what God will use to take you into the best season of your life. Yes, today and the times that follow could be the best yet. Go ahead and receive this thought by faith. Then walk into your new season of life, fully confident that God is on the throne and you are in His hands. As David wrote in Psalm 37:4, *"Delight yourself in the Lord."* When you do this, you will secure yourself and your emotions with the fact that you are in His hands. Tell yourself, and anyone who will listen, that God's awesome plan for your life has been set in motion and will surely come to pass. Believe it and watch God bring something amazing to you. It's a question of attitude. Make your confession and testimony effective by speaking words of faith and trust. God will be glorified. The devil will be horrified... and you will be filled with joy.

Today could be your day! Let go of the past and celebrate the transition. It's your key to tomorrow. When things are uncertain, I always take it as a cue to say, "I can't wait to see what God is going to do. It's going to be better than the best. Only He can do it and He loves me so much He most assuredly will!" After all, His word promises that *"He shall bring forth your righteousness as the light, And your justice as the noonday."* This Word is confirmed in many places in the Bible. My favorite is this one:

Proverbs 4:18-19 (NLT)

"The way of the righteous is like the first gleam of dawn, which shines ever brighter until the full light of day."

Imagine the potential for fruitfulness that one individual, a family, or a group of people carries within a transition from one season to the next. Transition inherently has the potential to present us with fresh opportunities and purposes. This tells us that transitions are as important as the seasons before and those that will come after. The lesson here is memorable. Our lives and the ways we behave have potential impact at any time, but could be of extreme significance within our transitions.

Are you presently in between seasons, anticipating a new one coming soon? Perhaps you are about to experience a transition you never expected. Consider what you could do to make and retain memories that will encourage, edify and motive you to press on with renewed zeal for God.

The Significance of Memories

FOUR
Making New Memories

My wife, Nancy's parents are both in their late eighties. Every day when she talks to each of them they tell her stories about their childhood and years past. Their memories of the old days are a significant part of their daily thoughts. These memories are precious and clearer to them than what happened yesterday. We often take our memories for granted and at times we fail to embrace the opportunity to make new memories. The times spent with the people who are most significant to their creation may disappear into the fog of our busy lives. It's up to us to deposit the memories formed as treasures in our hearts.

God touched my heart during a special time with one of our daughters, Robin. I had not seen her for quite a while. Here's what happened that birthed new memories that I have embraced as a treasure.

Significant New West Coast Memories

I had just returned from a week with my daughter, Robin. She lives on the west coast of the United States and I live on the east coast. It's a distance of about twenty-five hundred miles. It was a rather long trip that involved some inconvenience, and having to put my normal schedule on hold. It was worth every moment. I had not seen Robin in a number of years and we made some new and wonderful memories. This all occurred because she was facing a few days in the hospital and I had decided to be there for her. The time we spent together was God's gift to both of us.

When I got back home, and Robin was healed and back to her normal routine, it allowed me to reflect on what God was doing in my time with her. Much of it was simply showing me how precious she is to me and how valuable love is. I experienced the joy of getting reacquainted with her in ways that could only have come from God. I have not yet completely unpacked the memories I made, but among them was the intimate and intense presence of God throughout the week. My memories include the clear message that I can look forward to God's presence wherever I go. Regardless of the circumstances in which I may find myself, I can also look forward to making new memories that will come from giving of myself. This time with Robin became the engine of a transition from my previous relationship with her to one that now goes forward with an enriched quality it had not had before.

I previously quoted Jim Elliot, who said, "He is no fool who gives what he cannot keep to gain what he cannot lose."[8] Memories gained are completely worth the effort of giving away what cannot be kept. Within the limits of the time frames we are allotted, we can work sacrificially to make a difference in circumstances that will greatly matter to someone (especially those we love and about whom we care). A demonstration of love is real when it's given away. Otherwise, the memories of it won't become the catalyst for God to work something new and wonderful in ours or someone else's life. Having reflected on this, I have come up with a thought derived from the quote with which I began this paragraph.

> "He is unwise who keeps what he could have given and loses new memories he could have gained."

Memories - Yours, Theirs and God's

The moments in which memories are formed are seldom exclusive to one person. In the vast majority of the time, the memories we form are mutually experienced in the company of somebody else. The effect of these memories, be they good or not so good, won't exist in a vacuum. Our memories are like ripples from a stone thrown into a pond full of lily pads. When the stone hits the water, it sends out waves, one after the next. These meet the lily pads and the floating plants rock back and forth as they feel the effect or influence of the stone's energy. Let's apply this idea to our world in which we encounter others in the presence of God.

When you interact with someone, a relationship, whether

---

[8]Refer to Page 2: Elliot was a martyred missionary.

brief or for a lifetime, is formed. This occurs in the midst of a particular event or circumstance. Though we often fail to recognize it, memories are formed. It would be nice to recognize the presence of God in each moment we make our new memories. Of the two, three or more parties involved (us, others and God), only the Lord is sure to retain a perfect memory of the experience. He's always there, omnipresent and watching. In fact, the Bible tells us these experiences are being recorded in books and ultimately will be revealed, remembered and judged.

Revelation 20:11-13

"Then I saw a great white throne and Him who sat on it, from whose face the earth and the heaven fled away. And there was found no place for them. {12} And I saw the dead, small and great, standing before God, and books were opened. And another book was opened, which is the Book of Life. And the dead were judged according to their works, by the things which were written in the books... {13b} And they were judged, each one according to his works."

It's important to keep in mind that God considers memory-making moments important enough to record in the books that will be opened at Judgment Day. This ought to motivate us to guard and carefully consider our words and deeds. We should always make an effort to assure that the memories we make will be well pleasing to the Lord. He doesn't expect perfection from us, but He does expect us to try our best.

2 Corinthians 5:9

"Therefore we make it our aim, whether present or absent, to be well pleasing to Him."

Significant New East Coast Memories

I began the chapter by sharing my memories of a recent visit to my daughter Robin, on the west coast of the United States. A little more than two weeks later, following ministry I had finished in Brooklyn, New York, I traveled to see another of our daughters. Her name is Sarah. She lives near the east coast of the United States. Though I experienced the memories as they happened, I only began to organize them on my flight back home:

> Sarah has a wonderful husband, Juergen and four boys. At the time of this writing, the boys' ages range from four to fifteen. They are a great bunch of kids, each unique and special in his own way. I had not seen them for a couple years and they had grown far beyond my previous memories of them. My visit was a great time and an opportunity to seek out the blessings that accompanied this brief trip.

> I didn't realize it at the time, but God had a plan to take my relationship with Sarah to an even richer place. It had its parallels to my visit with Robin. The circumstances were very different, but as with my visit to Robin, God was working His divine plan to generate new and special memories in me from my brief stay at Sarah's.

Anyone raising four boys knows it takes a lot of energy. Sarah jokingly said it was like herding cats. As I observed her working with her boys, there were times when I think it was an accurate assessment. Even so, she did it with great love and inordinate patience. As I watched her, I saw the Jesus in her shining brightly. This confirmed the great respect and admiration I have for her. I think it even took it to a new level, if such a thing is possible.

Those few days with Sarah and her family continue to speak to me. They point me to something far beyond the animated behavior of Sarah's children and her patient and loving ability to direct their upbringing. As I reflect on my time there, I think beyond my memories of those times to the kinds of memories I hope to have left with them.

- Did the boys transition into a better understanding of who their grandfather is?
- Will I have had any influence on who each of them will want to become, because they will have some particular memories of my influence on them?
- Did they see enough Jesus in me to want more of Him?
- Will Sarah take comfort and have gained more wisdom from the times we sat and talked well into the night about things of God?

One thing is sure. There were memories made that will influence every one of us who was there. The effects of these memories will manifest far beyond those days at Sarah's house, as we transition into our individual futures. Another thing is equally sure. God was watching as we made all those new memories. I know beyond a doubt that they were filled with His highly significant purposes.

Significant Memories Yet To Be Made

Imagine the impact on those who recognize they are in the process of making significant new memories that will be of value to them and others they touch. These will become a library of experiences to be remembered and treasured.

There is a principle for every memory you will make that ought to be edifying and assuring. I'm speaking about God's promise that He will always be there with you. He said He would never allow you to journey through life alone. The Apostle Paul was clear when he wrote that nothing in God's creation has enough power to separate you from the Lord or His love.

Romans 8:35, 37-39

"Who shall separate us from the love of Christ? Shall tribulation, or distress, or persecution, or famine, or nakedness, or peril, or sword... {37} Yet in all these things we are more than conquerors through Him who loved us. {38} For I am persuaded that neither death nor life, nor angels nor principalities nor powers, nor things present nor things to come, {39} nor height nor depth, nor any other created thing, shall be able to separate us from the love of God which is in Christ Jesus our Lord."

With God, you are in the majority. You have the distinct

advantage. You are part of a plan that cannot be compromised or stopped as long as God is in it. This means that you can expect to make significant memories that will warm your heart, even when they include difficult and unexpected challenges.

FIVE

Among Your Most Valuable Memories: The Silence of the Lord

Nothing... Nothing... Nothing... POW![9]

Following a battle with cancer in which God healed me, and a time of convalescence in Florida, Nancy and I moved back to New York City. Our intention was to reestablish the church my illness had interrupted. We were living on Long Island, east of New York City, in a room that had been provided for us by a local church. It was a forty-five minute train ride into Manhattan. We were praying for a place to live in the city, and every day we were confessing in faith that God was going to make it happen.

After three months of prayer and preparation, our first service was coming in a few days. God remained silent and we had no answer to our prayers for a place to live in the city. We still had no direction on what to do. Our time in the little furnished room in Long Island was finished. We only had a short time to find somewhere else to live.

---

[9] A saying popularized by Pastor Dale Gentry, which many of us in ministry have learned is often truly indicative of God's way.

Nothing seemed right. Everywhere we looked was too expensive, too dumpy or too far from transportation into Manhattan, where we were establishing our new church. We were furiously going through the newspaper ads. Time was running out. We continued to confess that God would provide and we knew He was never late. We believed our confession, but were without an answer to our prayers. Anxiety was trying to rear its ugly head! Have you ever been there? Here's the rest of the story:

It was a Tuesday afternoon and we were returning from a long car ride to Albany, the state capitol, where we registered the new name of the church. It would be called "REACH Manhattan Fellowship." We decided to stop and see two lovely Jamaican ladies, Miss Lynn and Miss Daisy. They had been our landladies in our previous stay in New York until I became ill and we had to leave. The ladies lived in a lovely neighborhood in Queens. It was quiet, peaceful, and just a couple blocks from the Long Island Railroad, which provided a twenty-minute ride into Manhattan. We had really enjoyed living there before I was taken ill. As we were driving into the city I said to Nancy, "I wish we could just go back to our old neighborhood."

We decided to stop and say hello to the ladies. As we knocked on their door, Miss Daisy answered and said, "I have been trying to call you. There is a beautiful apartment just four doors down and I have spoken to the owner about you. Would you like to go over and see it?" Well, the lady offered us a great price because she knew who we were and wanted reliable tenants. So without so much as a phone call from the want ads, we were given exactly what we needed. God is a good God. He was silent until it was time for our faith to mature to the point when He spoke through Miss Daisy.

This memory of God's silence will always be with me. He spoke through a dear friend just when we needed it. From nothing came something, straight from the throne of heaven. "Nothing... Nothing... Nothing... POW!"

Psalm 28:1

A Psalm of David

"To You I will cry, O Lord my Rock:
Do not be silent to me,
Lest, if You are silent to me,
I become like those who go down to the pit."

It's inevitable that you will experience times in which you hunger for and may even be desperate to hear the voice of God. The uncertainty of these times can bring about doubt, fear or even panic. You can be tempted to forget that you have gotten as far as you have by trusting in the Lord and looking beyond the way things may naturally seem. When you begin to feel uncertainty in your emotions, recognize it's a significant signal to turn to what you know - that God has been faithful, is faithful and will always be faithful. Rest in this knowledge. Then, make the determination to stand on your trust in the Lord. When the Lord asked Peter if he was no longer going to follow Him, Peter replied, *"Where else would we go?"* The reality of our battles against emotions when God is silent is that there's nobody and nowhere else to turn to. These are times to say what you know, that Jesus is *"the Holy One of God."* Why would you turn anywhere else?

John 6:66-68 (NLT)

"At this point many of his disciples turned away and deserted him. {67} Then Jesus turned to the Twelve and asked, "Are you also going to leave?" {68} Simon Peter replied, "Lord, to whom would we go? You have the words that give eternal life. {69} We believe, and we know you are the Holy One of God."

We all face times when God is silent. When it seems we need to hear Him the most, He will often choose to let our present experiences speak to us. When this happens to me, and when all I hear is the deafening roar of silence, it becomes a signal to open my spiritual eyes and ears. It tells me to let my circumstances take me to the storehouse of biblical knowledge and understanding that lies within me.

Challenging, intimidating obstacles will come. It's easy to feel that we're not up to the challenge. I have wondered in amazement at the great faith others display as they walk confidently into the unknown. When I had to do the same, I may not have found it easy… but with determination, I built my faith by refusing to give doubt and unbelief a place in my heart. I also found that as I practiced my determination in the face of God's silence, it became the open door He had prepared for me so I could know His will, find His peace and receive His direction. This has happened to me more than once. In every case, He faithfully showed me *"which path to take."* Looking back, I have come to know that the silence of the Lord can function as a great generator of trust. Times when He was silent are among my most valuable memories. His silence can become among your best memories, too.

Proverbs 3:5-6 (NLT)

"Trust in the LORD with all your heart;
do not depend on your own understanding.
{6} Seek his will in all you do,
and he will show you which path to take."

Why Lord? Why Me Lord?

Have you ever asked God why things happened the way they did? Here's another common question we are tempted to ask: "Why did it have to be me?" These are questions that usually trigger His silence. I know this from more than one experience, in which I asked them. Invariably, in the midst of God's silence, I found my way beyond these two questions to the one He wanted me to ask. This is a question He guarantees to answer. It's the question, "Who are You, Lord." There you have it! It's the secret to hearing from God and obtaining His peace in every situation. Focus on who He is and He will give you the peace and comfort you need to press on without wavering or allowing fear and doubt to direct your path.

The best way to touch God is to seek Him before asking what He will do for you. It's all about your relationship with Him. I cannot explain this, but seeking Him often works best in the silence of your situation. He said, *"Be still and know that I am God"* (Psalm 46:10). I can testify with full confidence that His grace will be sufficient for every circumstance if you source it from Him quietly. Draw near to Him. Look only to Him. Worship Him, not His abilities or divine works. He is, after all, the author and finisher of our faith. He is our *"Abba Father."*

Romans 8:15-17a

"For you did not receive the spirit of bondage again to fear, but you received the Spirit of adoption by whom we cry out, "Abba, Father." {16} The Spirit Himself bears witness with our spirit that we are children of God, {17} and if children, then heirs - heirs of God and joint heirs with Christ..."

You may be facing silence in response to your own "Why?" questions. This is a good time to change your questions and your focus. I made a list years ago during my devotional times that will help bring you beyond the "Why?" and closer to the truth of "Who" He is.

God, In Me You Are...

The Bread of Life (John 6:35, 40, 51)

I want more of You, Jesus! I will hunger for You and more of Your righteousness!

The Light of the World (John 8:12)

Thank You for Your light, Jesus. I'll never walk in darkness!

The Door of the Sheep (John 10:7)

Lord, I am eternally in Your hands and under Your watchful eye. You are incredible! Fantastic!

The Good Shepherd (John 10:11)

I shall not want, nor fear the evils of this world. Lord, Your rod and staff will comfort and protect me. You never sleep nor slumber. I am safe and secure.

The Resurrection and the Life (John 11:25, 26)

I will spend eternity in never-ending joy and peace. What an exciting prospect! Thank You Jesus!

The Way, the Truth and the Life (John 14:6)

Lord, You provide my way, every day. You provide the truth that keeps me free. You provide my daily breath of life. You are the Guarantee of my eternity. Hallelujah!

The True Vine (John 15:5)

Jesus, I am eternally joined with You, and will be nourished forever. I am connected!

The Great I AM (John 8:58 and Exodus 3:14)

You are absolute in faithfulness and infinite in power. You are Ruler over all things. You love me more than can be fully described on this side of heaven. Awesome!

All My Stuff From God

It's been almost fifteen years now since I experienced the pain, sorrow, and ultimate victory in my bout with cancer while in New York City. God was faithful and healed me. I remember after recovering from my illness, I used to walk a certain street in my New York City neighborhood as part of my exercise regime. When I am feeling sorry for myself, or wishing I had some of the things others may enjoy, I remind myself of the encounter I had with God during one of those walks. The Lord did not speak audibly to me. Nobody else spoke for Him. Nevertheless, His message that day in New York City was loud and clear. God said, "Look around you at the beautiful street I have given you to walk with me every day." What a revelation this was to me! In one of my journals I recorded my response to what God spoke to my spirit that day. Here's what I wrote:

> "Thank you Lord for all these houses you have given me. They are so beautiful and full of life.
>
> Thank you Lord for these beautiful lawns and flowers by all my houses. I don't even have to care for them, but they are there for me to enjoy.
>
> Thank you Lord for all these beautiful cars you have given me. I can walk down the street and enjoy every one of them. I don't even have to wash and wax them or get them serviced.
>
> Thank you Lord for the nice day. It's not raining. The sun is shining and it feels good.
>
> Thank you Lord for providing the people of the church you have given us to pastor.
>
> Thank you Lord for all that you have given me to enjoy and experience. My cup is full!"

Let's finish the list of who I know God to be. In me He is…

The Hope of Glory (Colossians 1:27)

All the riches of Your glory are mine to experience. You have given them to me!

The Faithful Potter - The God of Peace (Hebrews 13:21)

Jesus, You are working in me to make me complete in every good work. I am so blessed!

"And Moved Into The Light"

"It's not what I don't see…
It's not what I don't hear.
It's not what I may feel…
It's not what I may fear.

Though troubles may approach me…
Though rumors may abound.
Though others may reproach me…
I will reject that sound.

Though weakness may encroach…
On my God-given strength.
Though sickness comes to cloak me…
In Christ I will remain.

It's not what may attack me…
It's not what I may lack.
It's not who may desert me…
It's not who turns his back.
Jesus is my Master…
My Lord, my Light, my Shield.
I wait for Him with patience…

To Him alone I yield.

I live for Him with confidence…
In spirit I am filled.
I live for Him with faithfulness…
His Kingdom I will build.

It's not what I don't see…
It's not what I don't hear.
It's not what I may feel…
It's not what I may fear.

I'm just moved by my Lord Jesus…
And moved into the light.
I'm just moved by grace and mercy…
My life in Him is right!

I wait for Him to speak…
Yet, His silence I may need.
I wait for Him to show me…
And then, I will succeed!
Amen!"

Dr. Bob Abramson

SIX

Among Your Most Valuable Memories: The Voice of the Lord

There are well over a thousand instances when the Bible uses the phrases, *"the Lord said"* or *"the Lord spoke."* God desires to communicate with His people. The Scriptures confirm this, especially when there is nowhere to go and no one else to whom we can turn. This occurs when we find ourselves in difficulty or trouble. It's equally important to understand that it also happens when opportunity knocks and we desire the Lord's direction.

A Divine Interruption

"and the Lord spoke to Moses."

Moses was living on the backside of the desert, minding his own business, when *"the Angel of the Lord appeared to him in a flame of fire from the midst of a bush."* Moses turned aside and there he met God. They had a conversation that occurred in a holy place, for holy purposes. Moses must have left that fateful meeting with the voice of the Lord ringing in his memories for the rest of his life. Here's part of the biblical narrative that began with God's call to Moses, changing his life forever:

Exodus 3:2-4, 7-10

"And the Angel of the Lord appeared to him in a flame of fire from the midst of a bush. So he looked, and behold, the bush was burning with fire, but the bush was not consumed. {3} Then Moses said, "I will now turn aside and see this great sight, why the bush does not burn." {4} So when the Lord saw that he turned aside to look, God called to him from the midst of the bush and said, "Moses, Moses!" And he said, "Here I am..." {7} And the Lord said: "I have surely seen the oppression of My people who are in Egypt, and have heard their cry because of their taskmasters, for I know their sorrows. {8} So I have come down to deliver them out of the hand of the Egyptians, and to bring them up from that land to a good and large land, to a land flowing with milk and honey, to the place of the Canaanites and the Hittites and the Amorites and the Perizzites and the Hivites and the Jebusites. {9} Now therefore, behold, the cry of the children of Israel has come to Me, and I have also seen the oppression with which the Egyptians oppress them. {10} Come now, therefore, and I will send you to Pharaoh that you may bring My people, the children of Israel, out of Egypt."

The Lord spoke and divinely interrupted Moses' life. Moses never expected or sought what God tasked him with. The interruption destroyed Moses' comfort zone. It upended the life with which he had become so content. Because of it, he was radically changed. It would have been difficult for Moses to leave the pleasantness of his pastoral life. However, the journey brought him to where he could fulfill his calling and subsequently become a blessing. God exchanged Moses' settled life for one that was so much more meaningful and eternally significant. He became the leader of a generation of God's people and brought them to freedom. It was an unsettling interruption that was God's divinely given gift.

The beautiful thing about divinely given interruptions is that they usually involve God's purposes for others. In addition, they end up being equally purposeful and significant for us. Be sure to look into the interruptions in your life (good or not so good) to find the purpose the Lord places in them. You will discover that the greatest gift within them will be the memories of what results from what God says to you. Don't let them pass you by. Hold them closely in your heart.

I have a dear friend, Pastor Glenn, who lives a thousand miles away. For years, we have spoken to each other on the telephone every Monday morning. I have found a steady supply of the voice of the Lord within the words we share. Usually our conversations are filled with experiences from the week that just passed. Recently, we talked about Glenn's wife and her journey back to health from a devastating illness. The healing was a great gift from God. What was unexpected was the gift contained in Glenn's memories of her progress that very week. Here's the story:

Glenn's wife was stricken with a mysterious illness that robbed her of her ability to function normally. She could no longer do the simple things a wife and grandmother loves to do. She could not walk on her own. She could not stand and do the dishes at the kitchen sink. She could not go out to lunch after church on Sunday, as they had done for years. My friend Glenn assured me he had heard the voice of the Lord saying he was to stand in faith, don't waver, and watch Him provide a complete restoration and healing.

My wife Nancy and I were praying daily for the Lord to miraculously touch Glenn's wife with His healing virtue. It was a tough spiritual battle that so many others had joined with us. We refused to settle for less than a complete healing. Many of us heard the Lord's voice, confirming what Glenn had heard. We prayed in agreement, asking in faith for that complete restoration of which God has spoken.

Every Monday for many months, I prayed in agreement with Glenn during our weekly phone calls. I am pleased to report that when we talked one particular Monday morning, I listened to what surely will always be one of my good friend's most valuable new memories. We all had celebrated her healing by faith, every step of the way. God had now moved to complete it. Here's what happened. She forgot to take her walker to church, which she normally needed to lean on to get around. It was a communion Sunday. When the pastor called for the congregation to come forward to receive the communion elements, she rose out of her pew, walked steadily to the altar without any help, received her communion elements, and walked back to the pew. She did it completely unassisted. God had spoken. We all believed it. She was healed!

The morning I received this report, Glenn had to cut short our phone conversation because he was taking his wife out to breakfast - without the walker! It gets even better. She's no longer taking pain pills. Then, he told me that they went to do an errand after church and he had her drive their car to get there. I believe he heard the voice of the Lord. I found his telephone testimonies in the weeks that followed to be even more powerful. God said it. God did it. By the stripes of the Lord Jesus she was healed. That's it!

The experience I just shared with you points us to an eight-part principle for how to respond to the voice of the Lord:

1. Listen.
2. Receive what God says.
3. Believe it, never wavering.
4. Behave like what God said is on its way.
5. Thank Him before you receive it.
6. Thank Him while you are receiving it.
7. Thank Him after you receive it.

8. Thank Him that He did not remain silent. Thank Him that He speaks miracles into existence.

I was having lunch with my wife, Nancy, and mentioned to her that I was in the process of writing this chapter on "The Voice of the Lord" and how His words can be among our most valuable memories. She reminded me that she had written a lesson on this subject and it was on our website. It took only a moment for me to hear the voice of the Lord. He said, "Take what Nancy has written, extract the wisdom, then fill out the chapter with it." What follows is my effort to be obedient to the Lord's voice. What Nancy has written should help you understand how the voice of the Lord works to take you to new memories of thanksgiving and perhaps even amazement.[10]

Hearing the Voice of God

Nancy Abramson

"How do we to start living lives that are more and more being led by the Spirit and not by our own desires or the standards of the world around us? The answer lies in building a relationship with the Holy Spirit. We learn to listen for and hear the voice of God. As we build a strong, ongoing daily relationship with the Holy Spirit, we become more and more sensitive to His voice speaking to our heart and giving us instruction and direction.

---

[10] I have edited for brevity and style the content of what Nancy wrote. For the complete unedited lesson, "Hearing the Voice of God," here is the link to her teaching on our website: http://www.mentoringministry.com/resources-and-materials/nancy-abramsons-teaching-resources.

Can every Christian Hear the Voice of God?

Yes. Every believer can hear the voice of God and be led by the Holy Spirit. If you know Jesus as your Lord and Savior, you have already heard and responded to the voice of the Holy Spirit. That's how you became a Christian.

John 16:8

"And when He has come, He will convict the world of sin, and of righteousness, and of judgment:"

The Holy Spirit's voice convicted you of your sin. His voice revealed to you that Jesus died for you, was resurrected, and is the Messiah. This was spiritual revelation that you received. No one can say that Christ is Lord apart from the Holy Spirit. Every born-again believer can hear the voice of God.

1 Corinthians 12:3 (NLT)

"So I want you to know how to discern what is truly from God: No one speaking by the Spirit of God can curse Jesus, and no one is able to say, "Jesus is Lord," except by the Holy Spirit."

My [Nancy's] Personal Testimony

1 Corinthians 3:16

"Do you not know that you are the temple of God and that the Spirit of God dwells in you?"

"1 Corinthians 3:16 has special meaning to me [Nancy]. When I was first saved, I had an inexplicable hunger for the Word of God. I immediately bought a Bible from the church bookstore. Every night after my children were in bed I would sit and read the Word. I was also a heavy smoker. I would sit at my dining room table with the Bible in one hand and a cigarette in the other hand, chain-smoking as I read. One evening I came across this Scripture in 1 Corinthians. It said that I was *"the temple of God"* and *"the Spirit of God dwells"* in me. Suddenly, a light bulb went on in my head. I looked at the Scripture, and looked at the cigarette and looked back at the Scripture again. Revelation hit me for the first time. I was putting smoke, tar and nicotine into the same body that God had come to live in! I put out the cigarette and instantly was delivered from my addiction. I never had another cigarette and never wanted one. Even though I was a brand new Christian, I was able to hear the Holy Spirit [the voice of the Lord] speaking to me through the Word."

One of the greatest gifts God gives us is a personal relationship with Him. He wants to have a vibrant, significant, on-going dialogue with us. He wants to hear from us and for us to hear from Him. God is ready to speak to you. Do you really want to hear the voice of God? It is a very personal question. You may say, "Yes, of course I do," but be aware that once you hear from Him, you have a responsibility to respond to what He says. Do you want to surrender your life to Him? Do you want to obey what He says? Do you trust Him enough to submit your life's decisions to His wisdom? You may be thinking, well of course I do, but think carefully about that.

Selective Listening

What if God says something to you that you don't like? Some people want to hear from God when it makes them feel good, or if it is something with which they agree. They want the good feelings, the promises for prosperity and good health, but they do not want to hear from God when it comes to forgiveness, or serving others. They want the joy of hearing from Him about their future and the good things He has in store for them, but they still want to hold on to their anger or bitterness. They want to prophesy or lay hands on the sick, but they like to gossip and judge people. They have selective listening when it comes to the voice of the Lord. We all are tempted to fall into this category when God asks us to do something we don't want to do. We say, "Is that really you Lord?" At times we say this, knowing deep down in our hearts that it's really God speaking to us.

[Possibly your most significant memories might be those made when you obeyed the voice of the Lord, even though it wasn't easy or pleasant. You may have found that your obedience proved to be among your most noteworthy decisions, because it honored God and fulfilled His will.][11]

Do you really want to hear from God all the time, in every situation? If so, tell Him that you want to hear His voice.

---

[11] Brackets denote Dr. Abramson's comments.

Tell Him you want to obey His commands and follow His direction. Make a decision right now to lead a Spirit-led life.

How do you recognize the voice of God?

Once you make the decision that you want to hear from God concerning every area of your life, how do you know for sure that you are hearing from God? In the Book of 1 Samuel, we read that young Samuel had never before heard the voice of God. When God spoke to him, he thought it was Eli speaking. Eli then gave Samuel instructions on what to do. Samuel obeyed and clearly heard the voice of the Lord.

1 Samuel 3:1-10, 16-19

"Then the boy Samuel ministered to the LORD before Eli. And the word of the LORD was rare in those days; there was no widespread revelation. {2} And it came to pass at that time, while Eli was lying down in his place, and when his eyes had begun to grow so dim that he could not see, {3} and before the lamp of God went out in the tabernacle of the LORD where the ark of God was, and while Samuel was lying down, {4} that the LORD called Samuel. And he answered, "Here I am!" {5} So he ran to Eli and said, "Here I am, for you called me." And he said, "I did not call; lie down again." And he went and lay down. {6} Then the LORD called yet again, "Samuel!" So Samuel arose and went to Eli, and

said, "Here I am, for you called me." He answered, "I did not call, my son; lie down again." {7} (Now Samuel did not yet know the LORD, nor was the word of the LORD yet revealed to him.) {8} And the LORD called Samuel again the third time. Then he arose and went to Eli, and said, "Here I am, for you did call me." Then Eli perceived that the LORD had called the boy. {9} Therefore Eli said to Samuel, "Go, lie down; and it shall be, if He calls you, that you must say, 'Speak, LORD, for Your servant hears.'" So Samuel went and lay down in his place. {10} Now the LORD came and stood and called as at other times, "Samuel! Samuel!" And Samuel answered, "Speak, for Your servant hears."

{16} Then Eli called Samuel and said, "Samuel, my son!" And he answered, "Here I am." {17} And he said, "What is the word that the Lord spoke to you? Please do not hide it from me. God do so to you, and more also, if you hide anything from me of all the things that He said to you." {18} Then Samuel told him everything, and hid nothing from him. And he said, "It is the LORD. Let Him do what seems good to Him." {19} So Samuel grew, and the LORD was with him and let none of his words fall to the ground."

If I called you on the telephone and you had never spoken to me before, you would not recognize my voice.

However, if I [Nancy] call my husband, he knows my voice right away because he has heard it so many times. It's the same with God. The longer you know Him the easier it is to hear and recognize His voice.

John 10:27 (NLT)

"My sheep recognize my voice; I know them, and they follow me."

Guidelines

1. The voice of God will always agree with His Word.

   The Lord speaks to us through His Word. By reading it we get to know His character, His ways, His promises and His commandments. Our minds become renewed so we can think the way God thinks. Then, we will better recognize and know His will. When you hear the voice of the Lord, it will always be in agreement with His written Word. God never contradicts Himself. Knowing the Bible makes it easier to recognize whether what seems to be God's voice is genuine.

Romans 12:2 (NLT)

"Don't copy the behavior and customs of this world, but let God transform you into a new person by changing the way you think. Then you will know what God wants you to do, and you will know how good and pleasing and perfect his will really is."

2. The voice of God invites us to walk closer to Him.

When the Holy Spirit speaks, what you hear will bring you closer to Him. When you walk closer to God, your life is more fruitful and you begin to act more and more like Jesus. The Apostle Paul experienced this firsthand and it's a model we all can follow.

Colossians 1:10

"that you may walk worthy of the Lord, fully pleasing Him, being fruitful in every good work and increasing in the knowledge of God;"

Ephesians 4:1-3

"I, therefore, the prisoner of the Lord, beseech you to walk worthy of the calling with which you were called, {2} with all lowliness and gentleness, with longsuffering, bearing with one another in love, {3} endeavoring to keep the unity of the Spirit in the bond of peace."

3. The voice of the Holy Spirit convicts us of sin, so we can repent and do what's right.

The Holy Spirit is our "Helper." He is always there for us, but He never forces us to do anything. He will show us the truth about what's right, but we must make the choice. We can choose either to do nothing, or to turn away from what's wrong while choosing to do what's right. The choice is ours. Will we respond to the voice of the Lord, reject a lukewarm or uncaring response and turn to what's right?

John 16:7-14

"Nevertheless I tell you the truth. It is to your advantage that I go away; for if I do not go away, the Helper will not come to you; but if I depart, I will send Him to you. {8} And when He has come, He will convict the world of sin, and of righteousness, and of judgment."

2 Timothy 3:16 (NLT)

"All Scripture is inspired by God and is useful to teach us what is true and to make us realize what is wrong in our lives. It straightens us out and teaches us to do what is right."

4. The voice of God brings wisdom and understanding.

There is wisdom that can only be received when it is spoken from above through the voice of the Lord. It comes through a spiritual voice that's normally spoken to God's people.

1 Corinthians 2:10-13 (NLT)

"But we know these things because God has revealed them to us by his Spirit, and his Spirit searches out everything and shows us even God's deep secrets. {11} No one can know what anyone else is really thinking except that person alone, and no one can know God's thoughts except God's own Spirit. {12} And God has actually given us his Spirit (not the world's spirit) so we can know the wonderful things God has freely given us. {13} When we tell you this,

we do not use words of human wisdom. We speak words given to us by the Spirit, using the Spirit's words to explain spiritual truths."

5. The voice of God brings peace to our hearts.

The Lord's voice will not cause His children confusion. [He desires that we walk in the assurance that our paths are peace-filled and we are moving ahead within His will. He will speak to us and bring clarity and guidance, as we listen to Him with our hearts.]

1 Corinthians 14:33

"For God is not the author of confusion but of peace, as in all the churches of the saints.""

- - - - -

The Voice of God Comes Through Others.

(Dr. Abramson's Testimony)

I was relaxing at home after church. It was one of those afternoons that I felt a bit at a loss because the seasons I ministered, while living overseas, seemed to be over. God's timing is amazing! At that very moment, I unexpectedly received a phone call from one of my twelve original Fijian students in the Christian Mission Fellowship School of Urban Missions. His name is Pastor Peceli Qarikau. In 1996, he had spent many evenings sitting on the floor of our home in Fiji, engrossed in my collection of Spurgeon's writings. When he graduated, I knew it was time to give him the collection of these books, which he has to this day.

As I spoke with Pastor Peceli, he told me of many of the apostolic works he and another of my original Fijian students, Pastor Emitai Ratalatala (his brother-in-law) had accomplished in the northern parts of Australia among the native Aboriginal People. I was so encouraged to hear his report. I recognized it really was a message from God, sent to encourage me.

Peceli and Emitai had accomplished so much. Hearing about it was wonderfully edifying. Even more so, the kind things he said about the legacy I had left to him were a gift that deeply touched and strengthened my heart. Peceli said he had embraced what I had taught. He also told me he continued to personally display the integrity he saw in me. He said the people to whom he brought the Gospel recognized this in his character and trusted him because of it. As I thought about this, I knew it was God's way of letting me know He was there with me and was pointing me to the fruitfulness I had, but don't often think about. Yes, I had heard from God.

How Do You Position Yourself to Hear from God?

Seek to know God more every day. Learn to listen more carefully. Life gets so busy at times that we forget to listen. We should have an ear open to the Holy Spirit throughout the day. Here are eight ways to do this more effectively.

1. Develop a love for His voice.
2. Get in the habit of starting conversations with Him.
3. Make it a steady, daily habit to worship the Lord.
4. Hunger for and depend on His presence.
5. Just simply love the Lord with your whole heart.
6. Obey what you hear Him say without hesitation.
7. Never doubt what you hear from the Holy Spirit. Just believe and behave accordingly. He will help you.
8. Seek the Holy Spirit for His timing to do what He's spoken."

John 6:63 (NLT)

"It is the Spirit who gives eternal life. Human effort accomplishes nothing and the very words I have spoken to you are spirit and life."

Significant Treasures

SEVEN

Dry Brooks, Unclean Ravens and Other Significant Treasures from God.

Hebrews 11:1 (NLT)

"Faith is the confidence that what we hope for will actually happen; it gives us assurance about things we cannot see."

Have you ever faced overwhelming discouragement because you put so much effort into trying to do God's will and found it sapped your strength, causing you to want to just go away and hide? Has your assessment of your efforts been that nothing of any consequence happened? Did you feel that you just couldn't see what would justify your efforts and motivate you to keep going?

Weariness and discouragement have been common experiences for those of us who wanted so much to make a difference. Yet, in trying to do so, we found it exhausting. This has been and remains a common issue for God's people throughout the ages. It's especially prevalent in Christian pastors and counselors who labor so diligently but often don't see the results they desire. I have had opportunities to minister to such people far too often. Many pastors have felt like much of their efforts went unappreciated by those they tried to help. Even more significant was that some of them didn't feel God appreciated what they had done. It seemed to them that their experiences were futile. Thankfully, God is in the business of turning what seems to us to be futile and wearying into a treasure of great worth, or as the Bible says, *"a pearl of great price."*

A Pearl of Great Price
A Treasure from God that's Beyond Measure

God never promised that serving Him would be easy or without cost. The Bible illustrates this point with so many examples of people who served God faithfully. For most of these people and many of us, it soon became apparent that answering God's call to serve includes times of weariness, discouragement, pain, and yes, even failure. However, in the end, we will look back and see the faithfulness of the Lord, knowing He was with us every step of the way. Recognizing His presence is a good start to understanding the significant value of what it means to walk with God in obedience and love.

Matthew 13:45-46

"Again, the Kingdom of Heaven is like a merchant on the lookout for choice pearls. {46} When he discovered a pearl of great value, he sold everything he owned and bought it!"

Jesus spoke this parable, likening the Kingdom of Heaven to a treasure worth everything the merchant had. The merchant did not consider it a sacrifice to sell everything to get that pearl. The parable points us to the time when we weigh all we have in this world against the worth of our heavenly citizenship. I have known people from many nations who loved their native countries and the cultural values and experiences they knew so well. They loved the people, the land, the food and so much more. Nevertheless, if you asked them to weigh these things against being a citizen of the Kingdom of Heaven, it would be no contest. Do you treasure your place in the Kingdom of Heaven? Is it your *"pearl of great price"*?

Significant Pearls of Great Price

A friend of mine who pastors a great church told me of an experience he recently had. His uncle had been the pastor of a church that had been special to my friend's family for generations. When his uncle was very close to death, he summoned my friend to his bedside. They had a conversation that became *"a pearl of great price"* for them to share with each other. Here's a paraphrase of what my friend told me:

> "I arrived in the hospital and sat at my uncle's bed. We were alone in the hospital room and he motioned to me to come very close to him. He said that he had something to say that he wanted tell me for many years. Then, he laid his hand gently on my head, expressed his love for me, and asked me to assume the mantle of caring for his church. It was an emotional moment that will always be special to me."

As I listened to this incredibly tender and meaningful story, I thought of how precious that moment was to my friend and his uncle. It became a *"pearl of great price."* It was truly a treasure beyond measurable worth. My friend's words caused me to think about what really matters in this life. This tender story affirmed to me that Jesus is my treasure. His gift of salvation to me is my treasure. My wife and family are my treasures. My friends and all those I have been a pastor to or mentored are my treasures. Finally, my call from God to spend these years serving Him is also a dear and invaluable treasure. Taken together, the Lord, His saving grace, the people He's given to me, and my call to serve, make up my personal basket of priceless pearls of great price. What's in your basket?

A Dry Brook and Unclean Ravens
(Raven Pearls)

What does the thought of a brook bring to mind? Of course, it's a picture of refreshingly pure flowing water moving through the landscape that God created. Now, think about ravens. They are large black birds that live in the wild by scavenging their food from dead animals. Because of this, they were unclean to the Israelites. Their scavenging habits made them filthy in the eyes of God's people.

The Bible tells us that the Prophet Elijah risked Ahab's wrath because he made a public habit of giving no respect to the king and his wife Jezebel. It came to pass that Elijah told Ahab there would be no rain in the land, except at his (Elijah's) word. This resulted in drought and famine (1

Kings 17:1). After Elijah spoke this to Ahab, God instructed him to hide from the wrath of the evil king by going to the Brook Cherith. There he would have pure water to drink and God would send ravens to bring him food. As a devout man of God, this would not have been very appetizing. It must have caused Elijah great consternation. Nevertheless, he obeyed the Lord. Twice a day Elijah drank the waters of the brook, as he ate the bread and meat the ravens brought him.

1 Kings 17:5-6

"So he went and did according to the word of the Lord, for he went and stayed by the Brook Cherith, which flows into the Jordan. {6} The ravens brought him bread and meat in the morning, and bread and meat in the evening; and he drank from the brook."

Priceless "Raven Pearls"

Even though he didn't go thirsty or hungry, it would have been disheartening for this holy man of God to depend on food from unclean birds. It would probably be accurate to say that the prophet did not consider ravens to be pearls of great price. After all, how could something unclean be a *"pearl of great price"*? That's the wrong question. The proper question is, "How could something from God be anything but a *"pearl of great price"*?" The ravens represented God's grace. Therefore, they were priceless. God's grace continues today, as it has throughout salvation history. The difficulty for us is to see things as God does.

The ravens were God's creation and acted on His behalf. They were carriers of grace. They were God's anointed pearls. They were "raven pearls." Elijah eventually found there was no price beyond which he would pay for their provision in his life. Then, it happened. *"The brook dried up because there had been no rain in the land."*

1 Kings 17:7

"And it happened after a while that the brook dried up, because there had been no rain in the land."

As you take the time to continue in these Scriptures, you will find a biblical principle worth remembering: God will not isolate you in a place of need and then walk away from you. The next two verses illustrate this principle.

1 Kings 17:8-9

"Then the word of the Lord came to him, saying, {9} "Arise, go to Zarephath, which belongs to Sidon, and dwell there. See, I have commanded a widow there to provide for you.""

Psalm 37 also speaks of this principle of God's faithful presence and provision. It's a timeless principle and you can depend on it today. God remains faithful. You may not always agree with His methods or what He asks you to do, but you can be confident that His plan is best and carries a successful outcome. It will be God's grace in action. It's a plan designed to take you further on "The Proven Track of Significance." You can count on it! David understood this and expressed it well in Psalm 37. Here's one verse that stands out as David's testimony to God's faithfulness.

Psalm 37:25

"I have been young, and now am old; Yet I have not seen the righteous forsaken, Nor his descendants begging bread."

We often have to remind ourselves to look through the lens of what our experiences have taught us. This will help us open the eyes of our understanding. Then we will remind ourselves of the priceless blessings of God's provision, which are purely the expression of His grace.

Pearls of Flour; Pearls of Oil - Priceless!

The narrative now continues with the story of two very different people who were brought together by the Holy Spirit. They were the Prophet Elijah and a destitute widow. Both received the Word of the Lord and both chose to trust Him. Both responded in obedience and faith to overcome what must have seemed utter darkness and despair. They moved ahead by faith. In the end, God flooded their lives with supernatural provision. Yes, it was the story of pearls of flour and pearls of oil - pearls of great price!

1 Kings 17:8-16

"Then the word of the Lord came to him, saying, {9} "Arise, go to Zarephath, which belongs to Sidon, and dwell there. See, I have commanded a widow there to provide for you." {10} So he arose and went to Zarephath. And when he came to the gate of the city, indeed a widow was there gathering sticks. And he called to her and said,

"Please bring me a little water in a cup, that I may drink." {11} And as she was going to get it, he called to her and said, "Please bring me a morsel of bread in your hand." {12} So she said, "As the Lord your God lives, I do not have bread, only a handful of flour in a bin, and a little oil in a jar; and see, I am gathering a couple of sticks that I may go in and prepare it for myself and my son, that we may eat it, and die."

{13} And Elijah said to her, "Do not fear; go and do as you have said, but make me a small cake from it first, and bring it to me; and afterward make some for yourself and your son. {14} For thus says the Lord God of Israel: 'The bin of flour shall not be used up, nor shall the jar of oil run dry, until the day the Lord sends rain on the earth.'"

{15} So she went away and did according to the word of Elijah; and she and he and her household ate for many days. {16} The bin of flour was not used up, nor did the jar of oil run dry, according to the word of the Lord which He spoke by Elijah."

Think about the times when you knew you were in the midst of a dark experience, but determined to move ahead by faith. You believed there would be a light waiting for you beyond your present darkness. This is an excellent way to understand faith in God. You just move ahead, knowing the light will come, even when you can't yet see it. Even your faith can be a *"pearl of great price."* Elijah knew this and the widow found it out, *"For thus says the Lord God of Israel: 'The bin of flour shall not be used up, nor shall the jar of oil run dry, until the day the Lord sends rain on the earth.'"*

In my trials and times of trouble (and I have had my share), God's Word has never failed me, nor could it. It consistently provided me the security of knowing our heavenly Father has his eyes on me every moment of my life. His love was, is, and will always be there. It's so much more powerful than the love a human father can have for his kids. God has the same love for you and He will take you through dark times into the light.

Nothing encourages my faith more than the experiences of others who believed the Word of God, acted accordingly and saw the Lord faithfully take them into the light. Even more encouraging is that the greatest *"pearl of great price"* is His love for you and me. Look to the cross and you will see what I mean. Allow God to turn your times of weariness and discouragement into treasures of significant worth as you walk with Him along "The Proven Track of Significance."

EIGHT

The Treasure of an "In Your Face" Moment

1 Kings 17:1

"And Elijah the Tishbite, of the inhabitants of Gilead, said to Ahab, "As the Lord God of Israel lives, before whom I stand, there shall not be dew nor rain these years, except at my word."

Let's allow the biblical narrative of the hostility between Elijah and Ahab to continue speaking to us. Ahab's gross idolatry and evil behavior so angered God that He sent Elijah to pronounce judgment on the king. As you saw in the previous chapter, the land Ahab ruled so ruthlessly dried up from lack of rain. Elijah declared that God had given him control of the rainfall and until he commanded it, there would be no moisture in the land. Not one drop would fall from the heavens!

Knowing Elijah as he did, Ahab realized the prophet's words foreshadowed a devastating drought and famine. The scriptural record testifies to this and clearly shows the increasing animosity the king and prophet had for each other. When Elijah stood before Ahab and spoke his prophecy, it was a significant "in your face" moment of bold faith that God's people will treasure forever.

The Scriptural record also tells us *"Ahab did more to*

provoke the Lord God of Israel to anger than all the kings of Israel who were before him." Ahab was not to be approached lightly. His anger normally bought dreadful results. This had no effect on Elijah's commitment to speak the words God sent him to deliver to the evil king. Elijah knew what we sometimes lose sight of, that with God, we are a majority and have nothing to fear. We only need to be strong and filled with the knowledge of whom it is we serve. Here's part of the Scriptural record of Ahab's blatant disregard for the Lord.

1 Kings 16:30-33

"Now Ahab the son of Omri did evil in the sight of the Lord, more than all who were before him. {31} And it came to pass, as though it had been a trivial thing for him to walk in the sins of Jeroboam the son of Nebat, that he took as wife Jezebel the daughter of Ethbaal, king of the Sidonians; and he went and served Baal and worshiped him. {32} Then he set up an altar for Baal in the temple of Baal, which he had built in Samaria. {33} And Ahab made a wooden image. Ahab did more to provoke the Lord God of Israel to anger than all the kings of Israel who were before him."

1 Kings 16:30-33 provides a revealing principle about all that's happening in the world around us today. It's apparent that many people in many cultures are doing whatever they feel like, never thinking about whether God approves. They have established personal moralities based

on whatever so called "truths" they have manufactured. They have no fear of the Lord. They act with great persecution toward those who voice any displeasure about their sinful behavior. This is how it was in Ahab's time. The evil king made the same mistake people make today. Ahab assumed he had impunity from judgment or punishment. Be assured that God sees everything. In *"that Day"*[12] when Christ returns, Ahab will have plenty of company, standing before the Lord, hearing Him pronounce His wrath on those who denied Him.

Thank God for grace. When you give your life to Jesus, and follow Him faithfully, His grace is sufficient. Your sins were nailed with His body on the cross. In *"that Day,"* you will stand before Him with great joy.

The Believer's Authority

1 Kings 17:1

"...As the Lord God of Israel lives, before whom I stand, there shall not be dew nor rain these years, except at my word."

When Elijah confronted this worst of all Israelite kings, he established more than just his authority to speak for God. He also established there was the most basic of differences between His God and the cold, dead images Ahab worshiped. Elijah's words, *"As the Lord God of Israel lives, before whom I stand,"* point to two distinct facts.

---

[12] Luke 21:34.

1. God, whom Elijah served, was, is and will always be the only true living God! Ahab's gods had never been alive, nor could they ever be. They were less than nothing. God alone is the omnipotent and only KING OF KINGS. He is far above all powers and authorities and is the true source of authority. All authority rests in Him and is granted by Him. He does not ask us to understand this, nor could we, with all the evil in the world. We can, however, believe what the Scriptures say. God's Word is true and applicable to us today. We ought to adjust our thinking so it aligns with that of the Lord Jesus Christ and agrees with His Word, below.

Philippians 2:5-11

"Let this mind be in you which was also in Christ Jesus, {6} who, being in the form of God, did not consider it robbery to be equal with God, {7} but made Himself of no reputation, taking the form of a bondservant, and coming in the likeness of men. {8} And being found in appearance as a man, He humbled Himself and became obedient to the point of death, even the death of the cross. {9} Therefore God also has highly exalted Him and given Him the name which is above every name, {10} that at the name of Jesus every knee should bow, of those in heaven, and of those on earth, and of those under the earth, {11} and that every tongue should confess that Jesus Christ is Lord, to the glory of God the Father."

Philippians Chapter 2 holds what's perhaps as defining a theological statement of Christ's authority as there is in the Bible. It's important to understand that Christ has absolute dominion and divine control. No power in heaven, on the earth or under the earth can successfully challenge or diminish His power. He is Lord above all. Do we understand why evil people do what they do? Of course not, except that it's a consequence of our fallen human nature and openness to demonic influence.

2. Elijah's prophetic declaration to Ahab immediately established that the prophet spoke for and served God alone. Ahab would have understood that Elijah's words, *"before whom I stand,"* meant he could not be intimidated by Ahab or any other man. Elijah's words were a direct, public affront and rebuke to Ahab. They would have been recognized as such by all who were there. Imagine how Ahab's anger was ignited. Here was God's prophet, humiliating this seemingly all-powerful king. Of course, God authorized Elijah's words. Therefore, we could say it was God speaking to Ahab through His servant, Elijah. It was an "in your face" moment. As we read these verses, they are a significant treasure for us, even today.

We can take an important lesson and an unfailing principle from Elijah's words: Serve God faithfully and He will be with you, protect you and give you a voice of authority to declare what's right, pleasing and purposeful in His sight. You speak for Him by simply saying what His Word says. Look into His Word for His voice. He will never contradict Himself. Use this gift of God's authority humbly and soberly. Your words, when spoken in the name of Jesus, and aligned with the Word of God, carry power to heal, deliver and assist you in operating in the particular spiritual gifts the Holy Spirit has given you.

God is the same today as He was in those distant days past. He still entrusts His faithful servants with a word to be spoken at the appropriate times and places. He will trust you with His Word. It will be fruitful if you allow your life to be an open book and a testimony to your trust in Him. He will put a word in your mouth and stand behind what you say. Now, that's a reassuring, very real faith-builder!

In the final part of his prophetic word to Ahab, which was *"there shall not be dew nor rain these years, except at my word,"* Elijah made it clear that the earth would remain parched and the heavens dry unless and until he prayed. The dew would return and the heavens would empty themselves of rain only if he asked God for this to happen. This prophetic word to Ahab was the Lord's assignment to Elijah. With it, the strength of Elijah's faith and commitment to God came to light. Ahab knew this man of God who confronted him was a force to be reckoned with. The authority behind the prophet's words emotionally stripped Ahab of the power he enjoyed as king. Ahab received his "in your face" moment.

Elijah was simply a man, serving God as we do. He was operating in the same divinely given gift of prophecy that we may receive today. James provided New Testament confirmation of this, confirming the historical accuracy of 1 Kings 17:1.

James 5:17-18 (NLT)

"Elijah was as human as we are, and yet when he prayed earnestly that no rain would fall, none fell for three and a half years! {18} Then, when he prayed again, the sky sent down rain and the earth began to yield its crops."

We should be greatly edified and assured that the same prophetic processes at work in Elijah have not been diminished or done away. As the Scriptures below confirm, they are still God's gift to His church.

1 Corinthians 12:10

"...to another the working of miracles, to another prophecy, to another discerning of spirits, to another different kinds of tongues, to another the interpretation of tongues."

1 Corinthians 13:2a

"And though I have the gift of prophecy, and understand all mysteries and all knowledge..."

1 Corinthians 14:1

"Pursue love, and desire spiritual gifts, but especially that you may prophesy."

God had given Elijah a powerfully significant and unusual assignment. The prophet had complete control over the climate. Imagine the trust the Lord had in him, and he had in the Lord! Imagine the responsibility! Imagine the opportunity! When God gives you a word to speak and the power to fulfill what you have spoken, you will make a difference is someone's life. As you choose to speak what the Master has put in your heart, do so carefully, obediently and with grace. It will become the devil's worst nightmare. It will become an "in your face" moment that will fall on Satan's plans.

Some Things Never Change.

Since the fall of Adam and Eve in the Garden of Eden, sin has made its presence felt and projected its power and evil intentions upon humanity. The battles we face have historic spiritual origins. The methods and schemes behind these battles are becoming more wicked and evil today than they have ever been. The limits have been completely removed. Sin has gone beyond just creeping into society. It has a firm hold on the power structures in the world and is using them as a platform to try to immerse us in wickedness. It's a war. This is happening for the purpose of trying to deny us the heritage, culture and freedoms we walk in as children of the Most High.

Ahab was representative of and controlled by the same devil who is behind all of today's wickedness. As evil as Ahab was, his primitive weapons and tools of destruction cannot compare to the sophisticated means available to the devil today. The stream of evil has swelled until it is a raging, overflowing torrent that threatens to drown us in it. We need to have that same "in your face' attitude that Elijah had. The prophet knew whom he served. There was nothing God's enemies could do to prevent Elijah from performing his assignment from the Lord.

Some things never change. We need that same attitude when it comes to the determination to live a holy life that demonstrates the presence and authority of God within us. History records a non-stop stream of believers who had this attitude. It began with the first Christians and has been the story of countless others, including a multitude of martyrs who died for their loyalty to Christ. There were Stephen, James, Peter, Paul and so many others, most of whose names we will never know this side of heaven. These people were not swallowed up in death and defeat. They had their victories. These victories will manifest fully when Jesus returns, riding on His magnificent white horse in the clouds. God's people will rise again with Him. Soon after, they will celebrate their victorious eternal future in Christ. He will deliver the ultimate "in your face" conclusion to evil, death, and the grave.

Standing Firm

The appropriate conclusion of this chapter, simply stated, is this: Have an "in your face" attitude towards Satan, sin and the social pressures that would try to influence you to compromise your testimony for Christ. Stand firm for what you believe in the face of every kind of carnal intimidation. Do not bend to political correctness or non-scriptural tolerance, religious or otherwise. These are simply sin, that society has relabeled as what's right. Let your determination to honor God's Word be strong. You may not be a prophet, but say what God says and He will honor it. Treasure your opportunities to stand for righteousness. Make a significant difference.

NINE

Treasures Hidden in Plain Sight

Family, Friends and Fellowship

I have a habit of looking for things at home but not seeing them when they are actually in full view. My wallet, my keys, a jacket or perhaps a book - all fall into this category. My wife Nancy often will graciously hand me these things without telling me how easy it should have been for me to find them. They are usually in plain sight, but somehow I seem to easily overlook them. Consequently, I have become used to the idea that more than occasionally I require help to find what should have been easy to see. My tendency to overlook the obvious is not a critical issue when I need to find a jacket, book or perhaps something I need to take with me while leaving our home. However, there are times when overlooking what's really important is significant. It may even be crucial. Let's rephrase that. There are times when overlooking "who" is really important among family, friends and others is significant.

Those who are important to us can be like hidden treasures. Too often, we walk right past our opportunities to spend time with them and find ways to be a blessing to them. Unlike the buried treasure we read about in pirate tales, treasured family, friends and other relationships may not wait forever to be discovered or rediscovered. Also, unlike a pirate's treasure, their worth is far greater than any earthly price. Their value is eternal. We all have neglected some of these relationships. We have allowed them to stay hidden and ignored until they decayed into far less than they should have been, or perhaps even into a complete loss. This ought not to have happened, nor should it happen any more.

Our relationships are truly treasures. They are gifts from God, right there waiting for us. What have you done with the treasures waiting for you? What will you do with them?

The Treasure of Family

Let's look at two categories of families. First there are those who are blood relatives or perhaps those who have been adopted into the family. Second, there is the family of God, filled with all our brothers and sisters in the Lord. Both types of families have immeasurable eternal value. Both are easily overlooked in the day-to-day activities of life. How do we get beyond this tendency not to see the obvious - that both categories of families are more precious than almost anything else we encounter in any given day? Finding the answer to this question is vital. It affects the fruitfulness of our lives and the sense of worth we ascribe to ourselves. It may also seriously impact the well-being of those whom we call family. This certainly bears thinking about, as life will prove to us that we cannot go back in time or take back what we did or failed to do.

The Treasure of Friends

We get a basic understanding of friendship from Jesus and His disciples. He lived with these men for over three years and said many significant things to them. One saying stands out. The Lord said it just prior to His arrest and crucifixion. His words placed his disciples in a special category, as it does us today. Here's what Jesus said.

John 15:15

"Greater love has no one than this, than to lay down one's life for his friends. {14} You are My friends if you do whatever I command you. {15} No longer do I call you servants, for a servant does not know what his master is doing; but I have called you friends, for all things that I heard from My Father I have made known to you."

To His disciples and to all of us who follow Him, Jesus is a Friend who is *"closer than a brother."*

Proverbs 18:24

"A man who has friends must himself be friendly, But there is a friend who sticks closer than a brother."

Consider the meaning of *"a friend who sticks closer than a brother."* This proverb is a slice of wisdom literature and has a significant lesson within it. If we apply it to our lives today, it teaches us that friendship is a reciprocal relationship. If we desire friends, we must fill the role of a friend. The latter part of Verse 24 teaches us that among our friends, there are certain ones who identify us as their treasures. These are people who will not allow distance or loss of commitment to come between them and their feelings for us. They are our treasures and we are theirs. In the family of God, they form covenant commitments with us (though often unspoken). They can be depended on to walk with us through the good times and bad. They imitate Christ, who calls us friends. To the Lord, friendship in His body is vital. The Apostle Paul had this in mind and confirmed it when he wrote, *"Imitate me just as I also imitate Christ"* (1 Corinthians 11:1).

The Treasure of Fellowship

Fellowship is of far-reaching significance for Christians. It goes into and beyond families, friends, church and other Christian organizations. It's what allows missionaries to go to distant places and instantly feel at home among those of common faith. It's also what allows these same missionaries to open lines of communication in order to break through barriers so they can bring the Gospel to the lost. It's how we gain acceptance with those who have yet to experience Jesus, so we can let our lights shine into the darkness in which they live. It's also one of the most overlooked desires, and yes, demands the Lord places upon each of us in our ordinary day-to-day lives.

The original New Testament Greek word for *"fellowship"* was *"koinonia."* Among its meanings are the concepts of communion and social interaction. God intends us to literally cling to each other in the spirit because of the importance He places on unity. This is for our protection, survival and blessings. We are to love one another as He loves us. *"Koinonia"* is a treasure that's supposed to be tightly packaged and corporately held within His church. It's foundational to effective fellowship.

Tools for Effective Christian Fellowship

It would be appropriate to begin with 1 John 1:1-4, in which we can see the biblical intent for fellowship. Then, we can look at the tools we need to be effective in our fellowship with each other.

1 John 1:1-4

"That which was from the beginning, which we have heard, which we have seen with our eyes, which we have looked upon, and our hands have handled, concerning the Word of life - {2} the life was manifested, and we have seen, and bear witness, and declare to you that eternal life which was with the Father and was manifested to us - {3} that which we have seen and heard we declare to you, that you also may have fellowship with us; and truly our fellowship is with the Father and with His Son Jesus Christ. {4} And these things we write to you that your joy may be full."

There are at least two principles written in this portion of John's epistle that show us the proper significance of Christian fellowship. In Verse 3, John writes that our fellowship with each other is to be wrapped in our fellowship with the Father and His Son Jesus. This is significant because, aware of it or not, the ways we conduct our times with each other always include the presence of God. We have no fellowship of any kind in a vacuum. God is the primary participant in all Christian fellowship. Therefore, it's important to keep our hearts open to Him as we open them to others in fellowship. The Holy Spirit is with us and He is listening. He is to be our Guide. He will help us judge our words and behaviors.

The second principle occurs in Verses 3-4, in which John tells us the Father and Jesus are the foundation of our fellowship, enabling us to do what's pleasing to them. This will result in the fullness of joy manifesting within us. It will be a reward for our God-directed, God-inclusive fellowship. Now, let's turn to some specific, significant tools available to us for effective fellowship.

Eight Significant Tools

Authentic Christian fellowship requires the demonstrated presence and priority of Christian love (*"agape"*). This imitates, as much as possible, the love Christ has for us. Therefore, the tools we employ to construct and maintain effective Christian fellowship must be found in what we know of Christ's love toward us. The Apostle Paul understood this. In 1 Corinthians 11:1, he encourages us (or perhaps it's a command) to become like the Lord in our words and deeds. Paul wrote to imitate him (and by inference, those like him) in the same ways he imitated Christ. It's often said, and rightly so, that imitation is the greatest form of flattery toward someone you look up to and want to become like.

As Paul continued his writings to the Corinthians, he endeavored to correct and thus enrich the ways they fellowshipped with each other. What we read in 1 Corinthians 13:4-8 gives us an opportunity to extract a list, containing eight positive elements of God's love. When applied to Christian fellowship, the list provides us with the tools to effectively construct and maintain this fellowship. This list will focus on the positives and bypass the negatives within these five verses of Chapter 13. Here are the Scriptures in the New Living Translation and then the list:

1 Corinthians 13:4-8 (NLT)

"Love is patient and kind. Love is not jealous or boastful or proud {5} or rude. It does not demand its own way. It is not irritable, and it keeps no record of being wronged. {6} It does not rejoice about injustice but rejoices whenever the truth wins out. {7} Love never gives up, never loses faith, is always hopeful, and endures through every circumstance. {8} Prophecy and speaking in unknown languages and special knowledge will become useless. But love will last forever!"

Love is:

1.	*"patient"*	Verse 4
2.	*"kind"*	Verse 4
3.	*"rejoices when truth wins out"*	Verse 6
4.	*"never gives up"*	Verse 7
5.	*"never loses faith"*	Verse 7
6.	*"is always hopeful"*	Verse 7

7. *"endures through every circumstance"*   Verse 7
8. *"lasts forever"* (Love is eternal.)   Verse 8

Let's combine these eight positive tools for effective Christian fellowship by putting them into a paraphrase:

> "God's kind of love (Christian love), at work in us, is patient and kind. It refuses to give up. It's founded on truth and rejoices when the truth wins out. It maintains an immovable faith in God and in those with whom we have relationships. Love is always hopeful of the best outcomes that concern the people we care about. In the midst of this faith and hope, our Christian love stands firm, enduring every circumstance. It will last through anything and everything because it is the imitation of Christ. It carries His own signature, written in His sacrificial blood on our hearts."[13]

As you can see, our tool kit of loving attitudes and actions gives us is a set of principles to build and maintain our relationships. Our list from the tool kit forms a dependable way to check our hearts and see if we are truly imitating Christ. He said He would build His church, but He's put the tools to do so in our hands and hearts.

Now, let's look at what does not belong in the tool kit. We can do this by listing the seven negatives in 1 Corinthians 13:4-8. Love is never constructed from these negative

---

[13] For an indepth look at 1 Corinthian 13, refer to "God's Kind of Love." It's available through http://www.mentoringministry.com/bookstore.

attitudes and actions that would keep us from imitating Christ. Here's the list of these negatives:

1. *"boastful"*   Verse 4
2. *"jealous"*   Verse 4
3. *"proud"*   Verse 4
4. *"rude"*   Verse 5
5. *"demand its own way"*   Verse 5
6. *"keeps* [a] *record of being wronged"*   Verse 5
7. *"rejoice in injustice"*   Verse 6

Let's construct another paraphrase from these negatives.

> "God's kind of love is never boastful. It harbors no jealousy and rejects the temptations of pride. It's not rude and is careful not to demand its own way. It walks in forgiveness because it keeps no record of the wrongs it experienced and the feelings they caused. It's never happy when something bad or unjust happens to another brother or sister in the Lord."

Now is the appropriate time to combine both paraphrases. Together they reveal a full picture of the beauty and value of acting as Christ would to construct and maintain Christian fellowship that will glorify God. These tools or principles, when combined, bring God's light on this immensely important subject. Here is the complete paraphrase:

> "God's kind of love (Christian love), at work in us, is patient and kind. It refuses to give up on loving the people of God. It's founded on truth

and rejoices when the truth wins out. It maintains an immovable faith in God and in those with whom we have relationships. Love is always hopeful of the best outcomes that concern the people we care about. In the midst of this faith and hope, our Christian love stands firm, enduring every circumstance. It will last through anything and everything, because it is the imitation of Christ. It carries His own signature, written in His sacrificial blood on our hearts.

God's kind of love is never boastful. It harbors no jealousy and rejects the temptations of pride. It's not rude and is careful not to demand its own way. It walks in forgiveness because it keeps no record of the wrongs it experienced and the feelings they caused. It's never happy when something bad or unjust happens to another brother or sister in the Lord."

There you have it. Let's all try to love as best as we can. God is faithful and will help us, through the Holy Spirit's loving presence and guidance. The treasure of family, friends and fellowship is beyond any earthly price. Though some elements of this treasure may have been hidden from you or perhaps partially neglected, now they can be clearly seen and acted upon. They are foundation stones to the Kingdom of Heaven. They are as valuable as any "pearl of great price"! Love is an immeasurably significant treasure. It describes the very nature of God. Scripture tells us *"God is love."* (1 John 4:8).

Matthew 13:45-46

"Again, the kingdom of heaven is like a merchant seeking beautiful pearls, {46} who, when he had found one pearl of great price, went and sold all that he had and bought it."

Thoughts on Treasures Once Hidden, But Now in Plain Sight

Because of my personal health history, I chart my weight and blood pressure. This helps me keep my doctor apprised of my current health. This is so he can monitor the medications I take and make any adjustments necessary to maintain the good state of health I enjoy. Imagine if we could chart how well we pay attention to our family, friends and the fellowship we have with them. With the help of the Holy Spirit, we can write memories of loving grace upon the hearts of our families and friends. They will become living testimonies of God's blessings through our fellowship with them. As this happens, we will also become demonstrations of God's love, enhancing and enriching our families and friends. We will see them as our priceless treasures - once hidden from us, but now significant and in plain sight.

TEN

The Greatest Treasure of Significance

One thing is of significance far beyond any others that might be found in your life. Its worth is incalculable. It leaves its imprint on an ongoing basis, even into eternity. It's the greatest treasure of significance - your relationship with the KING OF KINGS and LORD of LORDS, whose name is Jesus.

Significance is synonymous with fruitfulness. Jesus is the Vine. We are the branches. He said that without this relationship we have nothing, are nothing and can do nothing.[14] Our lives will have no lasting significance. With Him, we can be eternal difference makers. We should cherish this truth today and every tomorrow, without end.

The beauty of an eternal relationship with Christ, and its opportunities for significance, is that it's priceless. Its results carry the purpose of God and point us to His glory. Like His glory, your eternal relationship with Him, and the significance it holds, can't be measured in earthly terms. You have the potential to issue forth an unending stream of lovingkindness and tender mercies. You can be an endless explosion of His love. Your true significance will come

---

[14] John, Chapter 16.

when it reflects God's immeasurable love toward those you have touched. The more you give it, the more you realize it cannot be taken from you.

A Happy Song

As I searched for a fitting ending to the book, I believe the Holy Spirit took me back to another of my books, titled "God's Kind of Love." Near the end of that book, I shared these thoughts:

> "His [God's] love for you is not based on your behavior, thoughts, outward appearance, strengths, shortcomings or mistakes. God loves you just the way you are. The purpose of Jesus' loving sacrifice on the cross was to make a way for you to have access to God, so you can love Him both now and throughout eternity. When you accept Jesus as your Lord and Savior, nothing can separate you from His love."[15]

Then I quoted the ending two verses of Romans, Chapter 8. They tell us that nothing, absolutely nothing, can separate us from that greatest treasure, our relationship with God and His love. The International Children's Bible describes it this way in Verses 38-39:

> *"Yes, I am sure that nothing can separate us from the love God has for us. Not death, not life, not angels, not ruling spirits, nothing now, nothing in the future, no powers, nothing above us, nothing*

---

[15] "God's Kind of Love," P.133.

below us, or anything else in the whole world will ever be able to separate us from the love of God that is in Christ Jesus our Lord."

Will you hold tightly to this greatest treasure - your relationship with God and His love? Doing so will establish and empower your significance. Will you choose to pour out this love into your relationships with every chance you have to do so? Will you take the never-ending journey of discovery of this greatest treasure and what it means for those around you?

It's a journey that always begins with a decision to follow Jesus. If you have not done so, or if you have not cherished this most valuable of treasures as you could have, let this be your opportunity to commit or recommit to serving God. Make it a decision that leaves no room for turning back! God loves you so much that He gave His only Son to die for your redemption and eternal future. Let these words help you to make that commitment:

> *Father, in Jesus' name, I repent of my sin of unbelief. Please forgive me. I turn from my old ways and turn to the path You have called me to walk. I will love You, serve You, and follow You all the days of my eternal life. I now understand so well the treasure you have given me. Thank You for saving me, in Jesus' name. Amen.*

As I did to end my book "God's Kind of Love," let me encourage you with this timeless thought from Zephaniah 3:17.

Fill your heart, your life's journey and your destiny with God's kind of love. Then, you will walk through all your days, listening with gladness to your Savior's happy song of love. He sings it just for you.

Zephaniah 3:17 (NLT)

"For the LORD your God has arrived to live among you. He is a mighty savior. He will rejoice over you with great gladness. With his love, he will calm all your fears. He will exult over you by singing a happy song."

Never doubt that God is completely committed to travelling your life's journey with you. You can be as close to Him as a branch that draws its life from its vine, for He is the True Vine.[16] God's desire is that your footsteps will leave lasting imprints of significance long after you have passed into glory. Bring "The Greatest Treasure of Significance" to others. It will bring an eternal difference into their lives. Never lose sight of this: "He is wise who sees the significance of what should be cherished today without waiting for tomorrow."[17]

With every blessing,
and a happy song from God,
Dr. Bob Abramson

---

[16] John 15:1
[17] Page 2.

About Dr. Abramson

Dr. Abramson has extensive experience as a cross-cultural mentor and educator of those in the five-fold ministry. He and his wife Nancy have been pastors of international churches in New York City and the Fiji Islands in the South Pacific. He established or taught in Bible schools and ministry training centers in New Zealand, Fiji, Taiwan, Hong Kong, Malaysia, Europe and the United States. He provides free resources worldwide through his website, "Mentoring Ministry" (www.mentoringministry.com).

Dr. Abramson earned a Doctor of Ministry from Erskine Theological Seminary; a Masters in Religion from Liberty University, with additional post-graduate studies; and a Bachelor of Arts in the Bible with a minor in Systematic Theology from Southeastern University. He and his wife Nancy live in Lake Worth, Florida. They have five grown children and seven grandchildren.

Contact Dr. Abramson, at www.mentoringministry.com
or write him at Dr.Bob@mentoringministry.com

Dr. Abramson is the author of these books and resources:

- "Just a Little Bit More - The Heart of a Mentor"
  (Book and Workbook)
- "The Leadership Puzzle"
  (Two Workbooks and "The Facilitator's Manual")

- "Growing Together, Marriage Enrichment for Every Culture." (Book and Workbook)
- "Reflections - Spiritual Food for Thought," Volumes One-Three" (This is a series of devotional journals.)
- "Reflections - One Year Daily Devotional" (An inspirational daily devotional)
- "Stepping Stones" (100 illustrated, full color sermon outlines)
- "Moral Manhood - Swimming with the Sharks"
- "Focus on the Father - The Lord's Prayers"
- "God's Kind of Love - A Journey of the Heart"
- "The Fullness of the Holy Spirit In You, For You and With You"
- "A Kid in God's Tree House - A Devotional Commentary on Psalm 91"
- "Beyond the Rubble - Healing from a Broken Relationship"
- "The Proven Track of Success"
- "The Proven Track of Significance"

Dr. Abramson's next book will complete "The Proven Track" series. It will be titled "The Proven Track of Satisfaction."

Made in the USA
Charleston, SC
11 July 2015